THE
BROKEN
HEART

THE
BROKEN
HEART

APPLYING THE ATONEMENT
TO LIFE'S EXPERIENCES

BRUCE C. HAFEN

Deseret Book Company
Salt Lake City, Utah

Library of Congress Cataloging-in-Publication Data

Hafen, Bruce C.
    The broken heart / by Bruce C. Hafen.
      p.   cm.
    Includes bibliographical references and index.
    ISBN 0-87579-220-0 (hard)
    ISBN 1-57345-105-3 (paper)
    1. Atonement. 2. Mormon Church—Doctrines. 3. Church of Jesus Christ of Latter-day Saints—Doctrines. I. Title.
BX8643.A85H34   1989
232'.3—dc20   89-34628
                                  CIP

Printed in the United States of America   18961

10 9 8 7 6 5 4 3 2 1

For Marie

Contents

Acknowledgments

I wish to thank Marie Hafen, Jeanne Inouye, Michael Mosman, Donna Turley, and Jack Welch for reading an earlier version of this manuscript and for offering many worthwhile suggestions. I am also grateful to Lamar Berrett and Daniel Ludlow for their suggestions on the introduction.

Appreciation is also expressed to The Church of Jesus Christ of Latter-day Saints for permission to publish the introduction, chapter three, and chapter four, shorter versions of which have appeared or will appear in the *Ensign*; to the Church Educational System for the opportunity of presenting the material in the introduction to the 1988 New Testament Symposium for seminary and institute teachers; and to the people of Rexburg, Idaho and the Ricks College community, whose "peaceable walk with the children of men" (Moroni 7:4) taught my family and me about the doctrines of faith, hope, and charity through the Atonement of Jesus Christ.

"The Lord Jesus
died of a broken heart."
—*James E. Talmage*

"And ye shall offer
for a sacrifice unto me
a broken heart and a contrite spirit.
And whoso cometh unto me
with a broken heart
and a contrite spirit,
him will I baptize with fire
and with the Holy Ghost."
(3 Nephi 9:20.)

The Atonement Is Not Just for Sinners

After his return from the wilderness of temptation, Jesus read to a Sabbath congregation in Nazareth a passage from Isaiah 61 that stated a central theme of his ministry: "The Spirit of the Lord is upon me, because he hath anointed me to preach the gospel to the poor; he hath sent me to *heal the brokenhearted*, to preach deliverance to the captives, and recovering of sight to the blind, to set at liberty them that are bruised." (Luke 4:18; emphasis added.) In the Old Testament's continuation of this prophecy, Isaiah adds, "To appoint unto them that mourn in Zion, to give unto them *beauty for ashes*, the oil of joy for mourning, the garment of praise for the spirit of heaviness. . . . " (Isaiah 61:3; emphasis added.) After he had read to them, Jesus said to his audience, "This day is this scripture fulfilled in your ears." (Luke 4:21.)

By thus referring so broadly to the bruised and brokenhearted, the Savior pointed toward his eventual Atonement as the healing power not only for sin but also for carelessness, inadequacy, and the entire range of mortal bitterness. The Atonement is not just for sinners.

I believe there is in the Church today a compelling need for us to teach and understand the Atonement more fully than we do. Our need arises both from the erroneous perceptions of outsiders about our teachings and from our own sometimes narrow view about the reach of the Atonement in our lives.

1

For example, in its September 1, 1980, issue, *Newsweek* magazine carried a story entitled "What Mormons Believe." This article began by noting that "of all the religious sects to emerge out of nineteenth-century America" only the LDS Church "has developed into a major world-wide faith — and it is now gaining members at a rapid rate." The article then summarized some fundamental doctrines of the Church, noting in general that "their family values are mainstream America, but their theology is a radical conception of God — and Mrs. God."

Newsweek summarized our understanding of the Atonement in these words: "According to Mormon tradition, not only did Adam's fall make procreation possible, it also established the conditions for human freedom and moral choice. Unlike orthodox Christians, Mormons believe that men are born free of sin and earn their way to godhood by the proper exercise of free will, rather than through the grace of Jesus Christ. Thus Jesus' suffering and death in the Mormon view were brotherly acts of compassion, but they do not atone for the sins of others. For this reason, Mormons do not include the cross in their iconography nor do they place much emphasis on Easter."[1]

When I read this statement, I was appalled that a writer as sophisticated as *Newsweek*'s religion editor would miss the point of our core doctrine. I applauded when someone later wrote a published letter expressing dismay that this writer would have "spent as much time as he did among the Mormons" in preparation for that story, only to "come away with the conclusion that Mormons don't believe that the Atonement of Christ is efficacious for personal sins."[2]

But then came the *Newsweek* writer's provocative reply to this letter: "It seems that [the letter's author] doesn't understand the distinction between a book review and a magazine article. I did read several books of Mormon scripture and theology before writing the article. My intent, however, was *not* to review books but rather to report how representative members of the LDS Church describe and interpret their own traditions. . . . The point is to determine what doctrines of a church are genuinely infused into the lifeblood of its adherents."³

I remain deeply troubled that *Newsweek*'s readers across the country were left with a serious misimpression about the central teachings of the restored gospel. At the same time, the magazine writer's observation about Church members' actual understanding of the Atonement rings just true enough to leave me equally troubled about the level of our own doctrinal literacy. It is disturbing that some Latter-day Saints might convey incorrect ideas to members of other faiths; but in some ways it concerns me even more that this limited understanding might deny those same Latter-day Saints the reassurance and guidance they may desperately need at pivotal moments in their personal lives.

We should note, by the way, the irony of the accusation that the restored gospel doesn't take the Atonement seriously, given the enormous depth of the Book of Mormon's teachings on the Atonement compared with those of the New Testament. For example, as Elder Boyd K. Packer noted in his April 1988 conference talk on the Atonement, "Did you know that the word *atonement* appears only once in the English New Testament?" (That reference is in Romans 5:11.) "*Atonement*, of all words! It was not an unknown word, for it had been used much in the Old Testament in connection with the law of Moses." In the Book of Mormon, by contrast, "the word *atone* in form and tense appears fifty-five times."⁴ And beyond word usage, the Book of Mormon contains without question the most profound theological treatment of the Atonement found in any book now available on any shelf anywhere in the world.

Despite this remarkable truth about the Book of Mormon, we Latter-day Saints are, for the most part, only superficially acquainted with our own doctrines of grace, mercy, justice, and the Atonement. As an indication of our reluctance to consider the principle of grace, one researcher found only one serious article on grace in the periodicals published by the Church in the twenty-three years from 1961 through 1983.[5]

Perhaps some reasons exist for our reluctance to stress the doctrine of grace. The prophet Nephi wrote, "For we know that it is by grace that we are saved, *after all we can do.*" (2 Nephi 25:23; emphasis added.) Our natural inclination to think in categorical "either/or" terms makes us worry that a constant public emphasis on grace will lead some Church members to ignore the crucial "all we can do" in that two-part process. They might then accept—or appear to accept—what Elder Bruce R. McConkie once called the "second great heresy" of modern Christianity: "the doctrine that we are saved by grace alone, without works; . . . that we may be born again simply by confessing the Lord Jesus with our lips while we continue to live in our sins."[6]

Many Christians do take the idea of repentance seriously, but an overemphasis on grace can encourage the prevailing Christian view that we will be saved by grace no matter what we may do. Perhaps Nephi had this attitude in mind in describing those living in our time who would say, "If it so be that we are guilty, God will beat us with a few stripes, and at last we shall be saved in the kingdom of God." (2 Nephi 28:8.) At the extreme, this doctrine denies free will altogether, accepting the Calvinistic notion that God will "elect" those to be saved without regard to their conduct or even their preference.

In addition to the risk of this doctrinal error, there is a more practical logic to our fear that emphasizing God's side of the equation may justify our tendency not to do all we should. I was surprised on one occasion to hear a senior General Authority tell me something in a private conversation that allowed for greater flexibility on a particular issue than I had expected to hear. I told him how valuable I thought it would be if more members of the Church could hear his counsel, because what is said across the desk can so nicely clarify what is said over the pulpit. He replied that *private* counsel can be adapted to the attitudes and understanding of the person being counseled. If that same counsel were given publicly to an audience that included individuals of insufficient background or commitment, it might appear to give license to those whose needs require not more flexibility, but less.

For example, the person most in need of understanding the Savior's mercy is probably one who has worked himself to exhaustion in a sincere effort to repent, but who still believes his estrangement from God is permanent and hopeless. By contrast, some people come before a bishop feeling that the repentance process requires them to do little more than casually acknowledge the truth of an accusation. An increasing number of younger Church members even seem to believe they are entitled to "a few free ones" as they sow their wild oats and walk constantly along the edge of transgression. Constant emphasis on the availability of forgiveness can be counterproductive for those in these latter categories, suggesting — wrongly — to them that they can "live it up" now and repent easily later without harmful consequences.

Moreover, emphasizing God's mercy may lead some to believe they are entitled to divine protection against all of life's natural adversities. There is already enough theological difficulty for those who believe that their activity in the Church should somehow protect them from tragedy and sorrow. Our understanding of the Atonement is hardly a shield against sorrow; rather, it is a rich source of strength to deal productively with the disappointments and heartbreaks that form the deliberate fabric of mortal life. The gospel was given us to heal our pain, not to prevent it.

Having noted these reasons for caution, however, I sense that an increasing number of deeply committed Church members are weighed down beyond the breaking point with discouragement about their personal lives. When we habitually understate the meaning of the Atonement, we take more serious risks than simply leaving one another without comforting reassurances — for some may simply drop out of the race, worn out and beaten down with the harsh and untrue belief that they are just not celestial material.

The Savior himself was not concerned that he would give aid and comfort to backsliders or that he would seem to be soft on sin. Said he, "Come unto me, all ye that labour and are heavy laden, and I will give you rest.... For my yoke is easy, and my burden is light." (Matthew 11:28-30.) He spoke these words of comfort in the overall context of his demanding teachings about the strait and narrow way and the need to develop a love so pure that it would extinguish not only hatred, but lust and anger. He said his yoke is easy, but he asked for all our hearts.

His words do not describe an event or even simply an attitude, but a process; not the answer to a yes or no question, but an essay, written in the winding trail of our experience. Along that trail, he is not only aware of our limitations, he will also in due course compensate for them, "after all we can do." That, in *addition* to forgiveness for sin, is a crucial part of the Good News of the gospel, part of the Victory, part of the Atonement. For such a purpose each of us needs to take the Atonement more fully into the deep parts of our consciousness, even if there are some good reasons not to stress the role of grace excessively.

I wish now to summarize the elements of doctrine that apply the holy Atonement and its enabling grace to our lives. In this way I hope to illustrate how fully each of us needs the Lord's power and how earnestly he seeks to turn our mourning to joy, our blindness to sight, and our ashes to beauty.

When I think of the Savior all alone that night in Gethsemane, a solitary light shining in the vast darkness of cosmic evil, I think of the millions of people for whom he alone paid the full ransom. Then I recall Elder Neal A. Maxwell's phrase about "the awful arithmetic of the Atonement." The wonder of that event is clearly beyond our comprehension. As Elder Packer said, "How the Atonement was wrought, we do not know. No mortal watched as evil turned away and hid in shame before the light of that pure being."[7]

The first and most familiar elements of the Atonement relate to the transgression of Adam and Eve and to our personal sins. Because of the Fall, Adam and his children became subject to death, sin, and other characteristics of mortality that separated them from God. To allow mankind again to be "at one" with God, the eternal law of justice required compensation for these consequences of the Fall. The eternal law of mercy allowed the Savior to make that compensation fully through the great "at-one-ment,"[8] relieving Adam and his children of their unbearable burdens.

Somehow, through his sinless life, his genetic nature as the Only Begotten of the Father, and his willingness to drink the bitter cup of justice, the Lord Jesus Christ was able to atone *unconditionally* for the original sin of Adam and Eve and for the physical death, and to atone *conditionally* for the personal sins of all mankind.

The unconditional parts of the Atonement, those that assure our resurrection from physical death and that pay for Adam's transgression, require no further action on our part. They are the free gifts of unmerited divine grace. The conditional part, however, requires our repentance — part of "all we can do" — as the condition of applying mercy to our personal sins. We have been told that if we do not repent, we must suffer even as the Savior did to satisfy the demands of justice. (See D&C 19:15-17.)

I once wondered if those who refuse to repent but who then satisfy the law of justice by paying for their own sins are then worthy to enter the celestial kingdom. The answer is no. The entrance requirements for celestial life are simply higher than merely satisfying the law of justice. For that reason, paying for our sins will not bear the same fruit as repenting of our sins. Justice is a law of balance and order and it must be satisfied, either through our payment or his. But if we decline the Savior's invitation to let him carry our sins, and then satisfy justice by ourselves, we will not yet have experienced the complete rehabilitation that can occur through a combination of divine assistance and genuine repentance. Working together, those forces have the power permanently to change our hearts and our lives, preparing us for celestial life.

By analogy, the criminals who fill our prisons are not necessarily "rehabilitated" when they pay their debt to society by serving a fixed number of years. The payment of that debt may satisfy our sense of retribution, but only a positive process of character change can rehabilitate a lawbreaker.

The doctrines of mercy and repentance are rehabilitative, not retributive, in nature. The Savior asks for our repentance not merely to compensate him for paying our debt to justice, but also as a way of inducing us to undergo the process of development that will make our nature divine, giving us the capacity to live the celestial law. The "natural man" will remain an enemy to God forever — even after paying for his own sins — unless he also "becometh a saint through the atonement of Christ the Lord, and becometh as a child." (Mosiah 3:19.)

As King Benjamin here suggests, the Atonement does more than pay for our sins. It is also the agent through which we develop a saintly nature. When the Savior accepts our repentance and blesses us with his mercy, he restores our spiritual balance from a negative position to a neutral position. This complete process requires active faith, changes in our lives, and baptism or the meaningful renewal of baptismal covenants. But when we have taken these sometimes arduous steps, we are then only ready to *enter* the "strait and narrow path which leads to eternal life." (2 Nephi 31:17-18.)

Now we must consider an additional realm in becoming a saint through the Atonement — the process by which we move from the messy slate of sin through the clean slate of forgiveness to the beautifully full slate of a divine nature. There are many blessings of the Atonement in addition to the more familiar blessings of resurrection, the removal of original sin, and the forgiveness of our personal sins.

8

Let us consider first the general question of whether divine grace does more than compensate for sin as we normally think of it. As we consider this question, we will find that the blessings available to us are both closer and richer than we might have imagined.

The dictionary in the 1979 LDS edition of the King James Bible, under the heading "Grace," suggests that grace is needed not only because of our sins, but also because of our weaknesses and shortcomings: "It is through the grace of the Lord Jesus, made possible by his atoning sacrifice, that ... individuals, through faith in the atonement of Jesus Christ and repentance of their sins, receive strength and assistance to do good works. ... This grace is an enabling power ... [that is needed] in consequence of the fall of Adam and also because of man's weaknesses and shortcomings. However, grace cannot suffice without total effort on the part of the recipient."

Three of the most central figures in all of scripture — Adam, Eve, and Christ himself — illustrate the point that grace is needed to overcome limitations other than sin. These illustrations also suggest two significant ways in which divine grace can bless and help us, in addition to its compensation for our sins. Let us call these two categories *tasting the bitter* and *attaining divine perfection*.

Consider first the experience of Adam and Eve and the concept of tasting the bitter in order to prize the good. As best I can tell, the transgression in the Garden of Eden was not really a wrongful act of "sin," according to the meaning we usually give the term *sin*. For one thing, despite their obvious agency to choose, Adam and Eve were in a state of "innocence" in the Garden, not knowing good and evil as they did after the Fall. (See 2 Nephi 2:23.) Moreover, while their choice violated the command against partaking of the fruit, that choice was necessary to enable their obedience to the command to have children. Thus, what we call their "transgression" was a painful but correct, even eternally glorious, choice. For, as Eve later discovered, "Were it not for our transgression we never should

9

have had seed, and never should have known good and evil, and the joy of our redemption, and the eternal life which God giveth unto all the obedient." (Moses 5:11.)

Elder John A. Widtsoe once wrote that such statements by Adam and Eve "were not the words of sinners or of repentant sinners." Rather, the commandment not to eat the forbidden fruit was "a warning, . . . as if to say, if you do this thing, you will bring upon yourself a certain punishment; but do it if you choose." For this reason, "the choice they made raises Adam and Eve to pre-eminence among all who have come on earth." And "The 'Fall' and the consequent redeeming act of Jesus became the most glorious events in the history of mankind."[9]

Thus, the first time the Atonement applied to any human act, it applied to compensate for the harmful consequences of a choice that was more like a close judgment call than it was a true sin. Like Adam and Eve, though obviously on a smaller scale, we make many judgment-call choices that lead to pain or trouble — either for ourselves or for other people. Some of our judgments are wise, and some are not so wise. Think of accidents caused by carelessness, such as dozing at the wheel. They can have devastating effects, as tragic as deliberate violence. Think of unkind words and forgotten promises between spouses or among family members. Such incidents are never admirable, but not all of them are the result of conscious sin. Still, some of life's uglier consequences may flow from them.

Think also of the tragedy of what we might call a pure accident. I know of a man who ended the life of a college student at an intersection when the brakes on the man's pickup truck failed through no fault of his own. He returned to the scene of the accident alone, night after night, weeping and pleading with God to help him know what he could possibly do to make up for this terrible loss of life. "I can never forgive myself," he lamented. He felt heartrending guilt, but in what he had done he found neither true sin nor real relief.

We might think of the degree of our personal fault for the bad things that happen in our lives as a continuum ranging from sin to adversity, with the degree of our fault dropping from high at one end of the spectrum to zero at the other. At the "sin" end of the continuum, we bear grave responsibility for our deliberately wrongful actions and the suffering they cause. We bring the bitter fruits of sin fully upon ourselves. But at the other end of the spectrum, marked by "adversity," we may bear no responsibility at all. The bitterness of adversity may come to us, as it did to the man who owned the pickup and as it did to Job, regardless of our actual, conscious fault. Job's friends simply assumed that all bitterness is the result of fault or sin, so they insisted that Job's obedience would restore his prosperity. Job's wife believed his afflictions must be the result of God's weakness. But Job's own true perspective introduced a new thought to the Hebrew mind: We can experience trouble not only because of transgression but because it is a natural, even essential, part of life.[10]

Between the poles of sin and adversity along this fault-level continuum are such intermediate points as unwise choices and hasty judgments, in which it is often unclear just how much personal fault we bear for the bitter fruits we may taste or cause others to taste. Bitterness may taste the same, whatever its source, and it can destroy our peace, break our hearts, and separate us from God. We often — indeed usually — lack the power to compensate for all of the harmful effects of such bitter events. Could it be that the great "at-one-ment" of Christ could put back together the broken parts and give beauty to the ashes of experience such as this?

I am led to believe that it could, because tasting the bitter, in all its forms and with all the variety of its motivation, is so central to the mortal experience as to be a deliberate part of the great plan of life. The Lord taught Adam that his children would grow up in this lone and dreary world with sin conceiving in their hearts. But this consequence of the Fall was not a terrible mistake at all — on the contrary, it is the dimension that gives mortality its profound meaning. As the Lord said to Adam, "They taste the bitter, *that they may know to prize the good.*" (Moses 6:55; emphasis added.) Similarly, in modern revelation the Lord said, "And it must needs be that the devil should tempt the children of men, or they could not be agents unto themselves; for if they never should have bitter they could not know the sweet." (D&C 29:39.) Or, as he said to Joseph Smith when he was overcome with bitter darkness that was also not the result of his wrongdoing, "All these things shall give thee experience, and shall be for thy good." (D&C 122:7.)

The Lord taught Adam that the Atonement was given to him and to his children to heal the effects of tasting this bitterness—perhaps all of it. (See Moses 6:55-62.) The Savior extends this infinite power not just to bless any person who happens to have a need, or even just to answer prayers, but to fulfill the holy covenant arising from his deeply personal bond with those "few humble followers of Christ" (2 Nephi 28:14) whom he has ransomed with his blood. It is not just the Creation, and not just our being part of the Father's spirit family, that creates this sacred relationship between the Lord and his followers; it is the *Atonement.* Indeed, "mercy cometh because of the atonement." (Alma 42:23.) And it is "by virtue of the blood which I have spilt" that he pleads "before the Father" the cause of those who follow him. (D&C 38:4.) This healing power cleanses our spirits, upon condition of our repentance, when our souls are soiled with sin. It can also compensate for the effects of our sins upon others, when we are unable to make further restitution. The Atonement overcame the physical death and other effects of the Fall. It just might be that it also has power to sweeten the bitterness arising elsewhere in our lives—again, after all we can do ourselves to make compensation to the extent of our ability and our responsibility.

As Jacob taught the Nephites, "For behold, he suffereth the pains of all men, yea, the pains of every living creature, both men, women, and children, who belong to the family of Adam." (2 Nephi 9:21.) Of this statement Elder Maxwell wrote, "Since not all human sorrow and pain is connected to sin, the full intensiveness of the Atonement involved bearing our pains, infirmities, and sicknesses, as well as our sins."[11]

I have not attempted here to be definitive in marking the outer boundaries of the idea that the Atonement can heal us from the harmful consequences of our choices and experiences that do not result from deliberate wrongdoing. Surely at some point there are limits to that healing role; otherwise, the concept of Atonement could become trivialized and lose its essentially religious meaning. For instance, I would not suggest that this grand concept applies to every minor irritation or inconvenience of daily life, ranging from disappointments in the weather to unhappiness over a grade in school.

A sensible test for determining whether the Atonement applies might be the simple question of whether the experience in fact separates or estranges us from God. To make us "at-one" with God is, after all, the doctrine's purpose. Using that test, even the weather could be a source of serious religious estrangement for a farmer who loses everything to a flood or a drought; and a grade in school could be similarly critical if the grade flunks a student from an educational program he believes he was directed to enter in answer to his serious personal prayer.

Whatever may be the outer limits of the Atonement's reach, the essential point is that it reaches beyond conscious sin. We see the classic application of Atonement doctrine in the case of one who understands the difference between good and evil, yet consciously chooses evil in an act of rebellion against God. Such a person must return to God in earnest repentance to claim the blessing of atoning mercy. But many people sin in utter ignorance of how wrong their conduct is: "For there are many yet on the earth . . . who are blinded by the subtle craftiness of men . . . and who are only kept from the truth because they know not where to find it." (D&C 123:12.)

King Benjamin taught that the Atonement applies fully to ignorant transgression as well as to deliberate transgression, even though the degree of wrongful motive varies so widely between these two categories that they hardly seem sinful in the same sense: "His blood atoneth for the sins of those . . . who have died not knowing the will of God concerning them, or who have ignorantly sinned. But wo, wo unto him who knoweth that he rebelleth against God! For salvation cometh to none such except it be through repentance and faith on the Lord Jesus Christ." (Mosiah 3:11-12. See also 3 Nephi 6:18.)

This comparison suggests that the scriptures may use the term *sin* with different meanings in different contexts. For a further example of sin's various meanings, we have already seen that Adam and Eve's original sin was not a classic sin in the sense of an evil, knowing rebellion against God. Moreover, the ancient languages from which the Bible was translated used many terms with a variety of meanings that were all translated as *sin* in English language translations.

For instance, Bible scholars have established that our Old Testament uses the English word *sin* to translate Hebrew phrases that should more precisely have been interpreted as "missing the right point," or as describing "those who had lost their way" or those who "even with the best intentions were in difficulty."[12] Similarly, our Old Testament at times uses *sin* to describe what in Hebrew could be either wilfull "rebellion" or unintentional "error" that is "misguided but not unconditionally negligent or culpable."[13] Indeed, using terms we might call "sin" in English, some original Old Testament writers actually ascribe man's shortcomings to "the terrifying and tormenting" thought that "man cannot attain to God by his own striving because God withholds from him the ability to do so."[14]

Seeing Job taste mortality's bitterness, then, is only the beginning of his story. Whether one believes this bitterness came from Job's transgression, from God's withholding adequate ability from Job, from Satan's overpowering influence, or from God's love for Job, the bitterness estranged him from God. Whatever the causes or his personal motives, Job needed and found the healing blessing of "at-one-ment."

In addition, "the Christian view of sin" cannot be found in the classical Greek language. In the Greek conception, "guilt" and "sin" cover "everything from crime to harmless faults," not only "moral actions but also intellectual and artistic failings."[15] In Greek literature, guilt and suffering frequently flowed from man's ignorance, some of which was believed to be inherent in the mortal condition and some of which could be overcome with education. Yet, "for the Greeks . . . to become guilty and to suffer in consequence is simply to come to a deeper understanding of the world."[16]

It is by no means clear that the Atonement would apply to all these usages of the word *sin,* but it applies to many of them, especially when the *effects* of the choice or conduct are the same as the effects of evil-based sin—harm to ourselves or others and estrangement from God. In any case, the Atonement clearly applies to more acts than intentional rebellion. If it were concerned only with deliberately evil motives and intentions, it would not apply to those who "died not knowing the will of God concerning them, or who have ignorantly sinned." That "his blood atoneth" for these "sins" suggests that the Atonement's reach includes unintentional but harmful acts and consequences of many kinds. (See Mosiah 3:11.)

A higher degree of personal repentance is evidently required of "him who knoweth that he rebelleth against God" than would be required of one who violates divine law without such conscious fault, even though the Atonement applies in both cases. (See Mosiah 3:12.) It appears that the degree of repentance required may vary with the degree of conscious wrongdoing involved, because the repentance portion of Atonement doctrine is primarily concerned with changing a sinful heart. But the healing and compensating portions of the doctrine reach to include the effects of actions that were not necessarily motivated by knowing rebellion.

Having considered the application of grace to "tasting the bitter" in this broad sense, let us now consider the role of grace in our quest to attain divine perfection. Here we will see that the Lord's grace, unlocked by the Atonement, can perfect our imperfections: "By his grace ye may be perfect in Christ." (Moroni 10:32.) While much of the perfection process involves a cleansing from the contamination of sin and bitterness, there is an additional, affirmative dimension through which we acquire a Christlike nature, becoming perfect even as the Father and Son are perfect.

As an introductory illustration, consider the life and experience of the Savior himself, because his own development was marked by *his* receipt of the *Father's* grace. His experience shows us also that being free from sin is not quite the same as attaining divine perfection. Jesus lived without sin or blemish, which qualified him in that aspect to perform the Atonement for all mankind. Yet he also tasted of the bitterness of mortality in order to grow and develop: "Though he were a Son, yet learned he obedience by the things which he suffered; And *being made perfect*, he became the author of eternal salvation unto all them that obey him." (Hebrews 5:8-9; emphasis added.)

The Savior's personal experience is clarified by the witness of John, as contained in modern revelation. Note the role of the Father's grace in *his* development, which he in turn extends to his followers: "And I, John, saw that [Christ] received not of the fulness at the first, but received grace for grace . . . until he received a fulness." (D&C 93:12-13.) Now Christ himself speaks to us: "I give unto you these sayings that you may understand and know how to worship, and know what you worship, that you may come unto the Father in my name, and in due time receive of his fulness. For if you keep my commandments you shall receive of his fulness, and *be glorified in me as I am in the Father*; therefore, I say unto you, *you* shall receive grace for grace." (D&C 93:19-20; emphasis added.)

When the laws of justice and mercy are satisfied by the Atonement and by our repentance, we are, in effect, free from sin. But just as the sinless Christ was "made perfect" through

16

interaction with his Father's grace, so we must then move beyond the remission of sins to the perfection of a divine nature by a process involving grace.

Not long before he passed away, Elder Bruce R. McConkie visited Ricks College to deliver a devotional talk. As we drove together toward the campus from the airport, I asked Elder McConkie if he thought the concepts of grace and the Lord's Atonement had anything to do with the affirmative process of perfecting our nature — apart from the connection of those concepts with forgiveness of sin.

He said that is what the scriptures teach. Turning to the Doctrine and Covenants, he read aloud from Joseph Smith's description of those in the celestial kingdom: "These are they who are *just* men *made perfect* through Jesus the mediator of the new covenant, who wrought out this perfect atonement through the shedding of his own blood." (D&C 76:69; emphasis added.) In the same section we read this echo of the ninety-third section: "They are they . . . who have received of [the Father's] *fulness*." (D&C 76:56; emphasis added.) I thought about these ideas when Elder McConkie told the Ricks students later that day that the Atonement compensates for *all* the effects of the Fall and makes possible our inheritance of God's quality of life — eternal life.

At the very end of the Book of Mormon, Moroni describes this perfecting grace in a final, stirring invitation to his readers: "Yea, come unto Christ, and be perfected in him, and deny yourselves of all ungodliness; and if ye shall deny yourselves of all ungodliness, and love God with all your might, mind and strength, then is his grace sufficient for you, that by his grace ye may be perfect in Christ . . . And again, if ye by the grace of God are perfect in Christ, and deny not his power, then are ye sanctified in Christ by the grace of God, through the shedding of the blood of Christ, which is in the covenant of the Father." (Moroni 10:32-33.)

We know very little about this process of sanctification, but it is clear that we do not achieve perfection solely through our own efforts. Knowing just that much is enough to give us a new perspective. Because so many of us feel overwhelmed with the scriptural injunction to be perfect, the idea that divine grace is the final source of our perfection may seem too good to be true. That is how Christ's grace appears to those carrying the burden of truly serious sins. Honest people who carry the burden of being called "saints" may feel the same way, as they stumble daily through the discouraging debris of their obvious imperfections. But the gospel has good news not only for the serious transgressor, but for all who long to be better than they are. We truly become saints "through the atonement of Christ, the Lord," which, after all we can do, has power to help us become "as a child, submissive, meek, humble, patient, *full of love*." (Mosiah 3:19; emphasis added.)

The Atonement in some way, apparently through the Holy Ghost, makes possible the infusion of spiritual endowments that actually change and purify our nature, moving us toward that state of holiness or completeness we call eternal life or Godlike life. At that ultimate stage we will exhibit divine characteristics not just because we think we should but because that is the way we are.

The bestowal of the gift of charity is the clearest illustration of this process, as King Benjamin's phrase, "full of love," suggests. This love, the very "love which [the Lord] hast had for the children of men" (Ether 12:34), is not developed entirely by one's own power, even though our faithfulness is a necessary qualification to receive it. Rather, as Mormon so eloquently tells us in Moroni 7, charity is *"bestowed* upon" the "true followers" of Christ. Its source, like all other blessings of the Atonement, is the grace of God. Said Moroni, who was much preoccupied with this theme, "I prayed unto the Lord that he would give unto the Gentiles grace, that they might have charity." (Ether 12:36.)

The purpose of the endowment of charity is not only to cause an unselfish motivation for charitable acts toward other people, although that is a most valuable result. The ultimate additional purpose is to make Christ's followers *like him*: "He hath bestowed [this love] upon all who are true followers of his Son, Jesus Christ; that ye may become the sons of God; that when he shall appear *we shall be like him*." (Moroni 7:48; emphasis added.)

In his dream, Lehi felt the stirrings of true charity when he partook of the tree of life, which filled his soul with great joy and made him "desirous that [his] family should partake of it." (1 Nephi 8:12.) By eating the fruit of the tree of eternal life, Lehi tasted not only forgiveness, but also the nature of Christ. Charity is just one of the Savior's attributes, though it is central to his holy nature. And charity is only part of the total blessing. In its fulness, this "gift" of grace is eternal life — being fully like God — "the greatest of all the gifts of God." (D&C 14:7.) The term "at-one-ment" thus seems to mean not only being *with* God, but being *like* God.

Another divine endowment in this process is hope, which blesses us with the state of mind we need to deal with the gap between where we are and where we seek to be. It is the Comforter, the Holy Ghost, who fills us with this hope as the remission of our sins makes us lowly of heart and meek enough to receive him. (See Moroni 8:25-26.) I believe this endowment can literally fill our minds in a pure and permanent form with the kind of encouragement and confidence we might find in talking with a close friend who gives us perspective about a difficult problem. We go away from such a conversation with confidence that there is light at the end of our dark tunnels and somehow everything will be all right. That kind of hope can be literally life-sustaining when it is given us by the Savior, for the light at the end of life's darkest tunnels is the Light and the Life of the world.

Such a promise throws a wonderful lifeline to the increasing number of religious people who feel discouragement, stress, low self-esteem, and even depression. The Savior desires to save us from our inadequacies as well as our sins. Inadequacy is not the same as being sinful — we have far more control over the choice to sin than we may have over our innate capacity. We sometimes say that the Lord will not save us *in* our sins, but *from* them. However, it is quite possible that he will save us *in* our inadequacies as well as *from* them. A sense of falling short or falling down is not only natural but essential to the mortal experience. Still, after all we can do, the Atonement can fill that which is empty, straighten our bent parts, and make strong that which is weak.

The Savior's victory can compensate not only for our sins but also for our inadequacies; not only for our deliberate mistakes but also for our sins committed in ignorance, our errors of judgment, and our unavoidable imperfections. Our ultimate aspiration is more than being forgiven of sin — we seek to become holy, endowed affirmatively with Christlike attributes, at one with him, like him. Divine grace is the only source that can finally fulfill that aspiration, after all we can do.

I grieve for those who, in their admirable and sometimes blindly dogged sense of personal responsibility, believe that, in the quest for eternal life, the Atonement is there only to help big-time sinners, and that they, as everyday Mormons who just have to try harder, must "make it" on their own. The truth is not that *we* must make it on *our* own, but that *he* will make us *his* own.

Despite how little we know or can explain about these perfecting blessings of the Atonement, one other observation seems to hold true here as it does in applying the Atonement to the concept of sin. The scriptures suggest that the heresy of salvation by grace alone also applies to the personal developmental process. Thus, we will not be blessed with hope and charity and eternal life only for the asking. Rather, we must do the very best *we* can — even if that may not seem terribly impressive compared to a standard of flawless perfection. The important thing is that we *can* qualify, despite failures, bad judgments, wrong turns, and limited strength.

A few scriptural phrases can be pieced together that suggest the characteristics of those who are worthy of the sanctifying gifts. These phrases tell us more about attitude and commitment than they do about scoring points or never making mistakes. Consider just a brief sampling: "Pray unto the Father *with all the energy of heart.*" (Moroni 7:48; emphasis added.) Be "*true followers* of . . . Jesus Christ." (Moroni 7:48; emphasis added.) "Because of *meekness and lowliness of heart* cometh the visitation of the Holy Ghost, which . . . filleth with hope and perfect love." (Moroni 8:26; emphasis added.) See that ye "*bridle all your passions*, that ye may be filled with love." (Alma 38:12; emphasis added.) "If ye shall *deny yourselves of all ungodliness,* and love God with all *your* might, mind, and strength, *then* is his grace sufficient for *you.*" (Moroni 10:32; emphasis added.)

Rather than setting another discouragingly high standard, these invitations sound more like doing the best we can in the circumstances of our own lives. We need not apologize for the typical untidiness of those circumstances. It is their very lone and dreary nature that allows them to shape us as they do. It was never intended that we should partake of the tree of life and thereby gain full access to perfecting grace *before* we have stumbled and groped and learned all we can from the disappointments and surprises of this vale of tears. I suppose that is why the Lord guarded the way to the tree of life after Adam and Eve had partaken of the first tree: They needed the time and space and shaping purpose of mortality. (See Alma 42:3-5.) They needed to taste the bitter in order to "prize"—to appreciate, to understand, to grasp the *meaning* of—"the good." (See Moses 6:55.) Perhaps the essence of that good is the gift of eternal life, which we can only comprehend after we do all we can do. Until we are prepared in what may look like very imperfect ways to receive them, we are not ready for the gifts that perfect our nature.

In his dream of the tree of life, Lehi found himself in a dark and dreary wasteland and saw others surrounded by a great mist of darkness. The pathway home from this darkness was the way to the tree of life—the same tree, I suppose, as the one from which Adam and Eve were barred until they too had walked the trail where Lehi wandered. The path was marked by the iron rod, the word of God. Holding fast to this rod in the mists of darkness, we, as did Lehi, grope and move our way homeward. As we do, we are likely to find that the cold rod of iron will begin to feel in our hands as the warm, firm, loving hand of one who is literally pulling us along the way. He gives us strength enough to rescue us, warmth enough to tell us that home is not far away; and we summon our deepest resources to reciprocate with our own renewed energy until we are again "at one" in the arms of the Lord through the power of his great "at-one-ment."

Sometimes we talk about how important it is to be on the Lord's side. Perhaps we should talk more about how important it is that the Lord is on *our* side.

Sometimes we say that no other success can compensate for our failures in the home. And while it is true that no other success *of ours* can fully compensate, there is a success that compensates for all our failures, after all we can do in good faith. That success is the Atonement of Jesus Christ. By its power, we may arise from the ashes of life filled with incomprehensible beauty and joy.

According to an ancient legend, the Phoenix was a large and beautiful bird that lived hundreds, perhaps thousands, of years, then burned itself on a funeral pyre of its own making. A new Phoenix would rise from these very ashes with renewed youth and beauty, carry the remains of its father to the altar of the sun god, then return to soar for the rest of its life about the earth, the only bird of its kind. The long life of the Phoenix and its dramatic rebirth from its father's ashes made it a symbol in the ancient world of both immortality and spiritual rebirth.

Each of us will taste the bitter ashes of life, from sin and neglect to sorrow and disappointment. But the Atonement of Christ can lift us up in beauty, not only from our own ashes but also from the ashes of him who fathers the rebirth of our

22

spirits. We then soar toward the sun on the wings of a sure promise of immortality and eternal life. Thus may we be lifted up, not only at the end of life but in each day of our lives.

"*Hast thou not known? hast thou not heard*, that the everlasting God, the Lord, the Creator of the ends of the earth . . . giveth power to the faint; and to them that have no might he increaseth strength. But they that wait upon the Lord shall renew their strength; they shall mount up with wings as eagles; they shall run, and not be weary; and they shall walk, and not faint." (Isaiah 40:28-29, 31; emphasis added.)

Prologue

I. *About this Book*

This book *applies* the doctrines of the Atonement to some common elements of human experience. Thus it is more a practical book than a doctrinal one.

Still, I believe with Oliver Wendell Holmes that nothing is more practical than a good theory. The "good theory" in this case is the majestic doctrine that, as explained in the third article of faith, "through the Atonement of Christ, all mankind may be saved, by obedience to the laws and ordinances of the gospel." No idea is more philosophically profound than the idea of the Atonement; yet no idea is more intensely practical. This idea is so practical that it is a matter of life and death, in every sense of both terms. But it is also an idea that applies to all of mortal experience between life and death, especially the common but often wrenching life experiences that seem to separate us from God. For anyone who seeks meaning and purpose in life, nothing would be more practical than a sound understanding of this good theory.

The following chapters proceed from the doctrinal framework sketched in the Introduction and will develop many of the themes introduced there. That framework views the Atonement in broad terms, terms that are rich and packed with many unexplored implications. I make no claim to having fully re-searched and developed the theological issues this framework raises. I am acquainted enough with scholarly methods to have some idea about the scope and the rigor required to complete such a project, and I believe it is a project worth doing. But I have not done it here; that is a book for someone else on another day.

Some day I hope that others will write more about the Atonement theology of the restored gospel, if only to lead readers to the primary sources of that theology in the scriptures. Students of the Christian scriptures in all faiths cry out to grasp the grand secrets of the Atonement, which can unlock the further mysteries of man's nature and life's purpose. If only they could know what truths lie buried before their eyes in the plain and precious language of the Book of Mormon. These truths are in some sense inaccessible to those whose tools of language and discourse are limited to the terms of art em-bodied in the academic and jargon-laden discipline of contem-porary Christian theology. Great revelations—literally—await those who will let the Book of Mormon speak for itself about its central message, Christ's Atonement, "according to the plain-ness which is in the Lamb of God." (1 Nephi 13:29.)

This book is intentionally modest in scope and conversa-tional in tone. The doctrines of the Atonement are always relevant to these chapters but are not always on center stage. At times the Atonement acts here only as a backdrop, a source of quiet but sure perspective.

I write here to adults and young adults in the Church as a general audience. Many of my illustrations refer to the ex-perience of college-age young people, but that is only because all of us naturally draw upon our own experience. My expe-rience over the past twenty years has been primarily among the students and faculty at Brigham Young University and Ricks College. But these people are, I find, a cross section of the larger Church membership, and in that sense their experience reflects the common experiences of most Church members.

My viewpoint in these pages is not the panoramic vision of an authorized spokesman; rather, mine is the view from the trenches, where each of us seeks to connect our worn threads of life's tapestry with the vast, overall design. I love the characteristic of Church membership that lets us all speak to one another in a shared conversation that reflects our common search to know how we should live as Latter-day Saints — not always because we are sure we have the answers, but because we share a bond of brotherhood with those for whom the questions mean so much.

Just a word about titles and metaphors. *The Broken Heart* has a double meaning: first, the breaking of Christ's heart at the moment of his death on the cross, when he voluntarily gave up his life in the final act of the Atonement's drama; second, the broken heart and contrite spirit the Savior asks each of us to place before him on the altar of sacrifice. Through the breaking of his heart and ours in these two interactive senses, the full blessings of the Atonement are realized in our individual lives.

I thought once about a different title for the book, perhaps "After All We Can Do," from Nephi's memorable statement that "it is by grace that we are saved, after all we can do." (2 Nephi 25:23.) Much of the book does focus on "all we can do" as well as on the way the Savior lifts us up "after" we do all we can. But the potent symbolism of the broken heart, his and ours, has a special appeal, pointing toward the blessings of the Atonement in a way that binds our hearts to his. The present title also carries echoes of a companion volume, *The Believing Heart*, which deals with the process of faith that prepares us to receive the Atonement.

Following the introduction and the prologue, the book's chapters are organized around two additional symbols: first, the tree of the knowledge of good and evil; and second, the tree of life. These two trees have a definite and powerful meaning in the teachings of the temple and the scriptures regarding the Fall, the Atonement, and our return to God's presence.

They also link our personal experience with the experience of Adam and Eve in ways that illuminate the connections between the Atonement and our own journey through mortality.

II. The Light in the Darkness

Thirty-four years after the birth of Christ, a great and terrible storm arose in the lands of the Nephite people. Never before had such a storm swept over those lands. The whole earth shook over vast spaces. Entire cities caught fire, collapsed into the sea, and were buried under upheaved mountains. The face of all the land was torn apart and deformed. Many of the people lost their lives; those who were spared wailed in grief.

After the awful storm, a thick and frightening vapor of darkness covered the land. So black was the darkness that the surviving inhabitants could make no light at all with candles or fire, and the sun and stars hid their light for three days behind this suffocating veil of darkness. The people wept and howled and mourned.

Suddenly a voice pierced the dreadful darkness.

The people trembled in terror, and they strained their ears in the thick black night, desperate to grasp the words of the voice. They listened fervently, and they heard:

"I am the light and the life of the world. I am Alpha and Omega, the beginning and the end. And ye shall offer up unto me no more the shedding of blood; yea, your sacrifices and your burnt offerings shall be done away. . . . And ye shall offer for a sacrifice unto me a broken heart and a contrite spirit." (3 Nephi 9:18-20.)

It was the voice of Jesus Christ, whom the prophets testified would come into the world. He had drunk the bitter cup that the Father gave him. His heart was broken, and his Atonement was now complete. The light of heaven thus pierced the darkness of the world.

He asked the people who wandered in the dark night to offer unto him the personal sacrifice of a broken heart. And when they came unto him in this manner, he gave them light in the darkness of their lives.

III. The Two Trees

We shall not cease from exploration
And the end of all our exploring
Will be to arrive where we started
And know the place for the first time.[1]

Life is a school, a place for us to learn and grow. Our Teacher and Headmaster has placed us on the earth in a risk-filled environment called mortality. Here we may *learn* what we must know and *become* what we must be, not only to live with him someday, but to be *like him.*

To learn these profound lessons of life, we must undergo many experiences that subject us to the sorrow and contamination of a lone and dreary world. These experiences may include sin, but they also include undeserved pain, disappointment, and adversity. Every one of us will taste some bitter mixture of these forces. We must taste a measure of the bitter in order to prize the sweet.

But how, then, can we overcome the ill effects and consequences of this necessary contamination? The blessed news of the gospel is that the Atonement of Jesus Christ can purify us from all uncleanness and sweeten all the bitterness we taste. The Atonement not only pays for our sins, it heals our wounds — the self-inflicted ones and those inflicted from sources beyond our control. The Atonement also completes the process of our learning by perfecting our nature and making us whole. In this way, Christ's Atonement makes us as he is. It is the ultimate source of our forgiveness, our perfection, and our peace of mind.

In the beginning, the Lord God taught this vision of life's nature and purpose to Adam and Eve. To symbolize these teachings, he placed two trees in the Garden of Eden: *the tree of knowledge* and *the tree of life*. The fruit of the first tree seemed desirable, but it became bitter as it led to the knowledge of good and evil. The second tree was sweet, and it led to a fulness of Godlike life. We, like Adam and Eve, taste the bitter fruit of the first tree that we may know to prize the sweet fruit of the second tree.

The *tree of knowledge* (learning through mortal, sometimes bitter, experience) and the *tree of life* (the Father's sweet bestowal of forgiveness and a divine character) are *both* necessary for us to find fulfillment and meaning. Neither tree — neither force — is sufficient unless completed by the other.

The mortal learning experience, represented by the *tree of knowledge*, is so necessary that God placed cherubim and a flaming sword to guard the way of the *tree of life* until Adam and Eve completed, and we, their posterity, complete this preparatory schooling. Our tutorial is the gospel, a schoolmaster that brings us to Christ. But he cannot fully receive us and give us the gift of celestial life — partaking of God's very nature — until we have *learned by our own experience* to distinguish good from evil. In multiplied sorrow we must bring forth children. We must walk the earth through sharp thorns and poison thistles. The ground is cursed for our sakes. By the sweat of our faces must we eat bread until we return to the ground from whence we were taken.

This treacherous path led Adam and Eve through the valley of death and pain. It weighed them down with the toil of earthly experience, until they knelt before God in the depths of humility. Through faithful obedience and sacrifice, they *learned*, they repented, and they reached out to God through the veil of mortality with all the energy of their hearts.

Thus the *tree of knowledge* symbolizes the entire process by which Adam and Eve — and we — learn through the dreary loneliness of earthly experience. Partaking of the forbidden fruit was only the beginning of that process.

Over time Adam and Eve endured faithfully, until one day they began to grasp the joy of their redemption. This was the day when the Savior began to lift them up in reverent humility. By then their hearts were broken and their spirits contrite in two ways: first, their sorrow for their sins, and second, their courageous response to the natural adversity of the lone and dreary world. Then at last the Good Shepherd placed them on his shoulder and carried them homeward to the fruits of his love through the power of his precious Atonement, cleansed and perfected from the ill effects of all mortal bitterness.

Our Savior's sanctifying power is represented by the *tree of life*. Without that power, there is no life, only death and timeless despair. Had they never partaken of this second tree, Adam and Eve would have wandered in their quest for knowledge into a path of endless misery. This result would have fulfilled what Satan intended when he tempted them in the garden to seek knowledge without obedience, for he seeks that all might be miserable like unto himself.

Adam and Eve began the lifelong process of seeking after the fruit of the *tree of life* when, once their eyes were opened, they refused to worship Satan and chose, rather, to plant the seed of faith in the Lord Jesus Christ. They then nourished their small seedling with much care, so that it would not wither in the scorching heat of opposition. When finally, after great patience and diligence, they plucked and tasted the fruit of the *tree of life*, it was sweet above all that is sweet and pure above all that is pure; for it represents the pure love of God, the most desirable of all things, made possible through the infinite Atonement of him who died of a broken heart.

He, too, knew of toil, and sweat, and sorrow, for Man of Sorrows was his name. In the days of his flesh, he prayed with strong crying and tears unto him that was able to save him from death. He was despised and rejected of men. He was acquainted with grief and bruised for our iniquities. Having himself suffered temptation, he can succor those who are tempted. For his followers, the sweetest moment of his life was when he drank the bitter cup.

31

To lay claim to the Savior's sacrifice, we, like Adam and Eve, must also obey and sacrifice. We must bring an offering that in some way approximates his own suffering — the sacrifice of a broken heart and a contrite spirit.

The Savior's completion of his Atonement changed the nature of the law of sacrifice in a way that requires that our hearts be broken. Formerly, the Old Testament's law of sacrifice required literal animal sacrifices and burnt offerings. But after the Atonement fulfilled the law of Moses, Jesus explained to the Nephites that they should do away with animal sacrifices. Henceforth, he taught that whoever would come unto him with a broken heart and a contrite spirit, he would baptize with fire and with the Holy Ghost.

Elder James E. Talmage believed that the physiological cause of Christ's death was, literally, a broken heart. This element in our Lord's sacrifice suggests two differences between animal sacrifices and the sacrifice of a broken heart. First is the difference between offering one of our possessions, such as an animal, and offering our own hearts. Second, one who offers an unblemished animal, the firstling of a flock, acts in similitude of the *Father's* sacrifice of his unblemished, firstborn Son. By contrast, one who offers his own broken heart acts in similitude of the *Son's* terribly personal sacrifice of himself. Thus, the figurative breaking of our own hearts, represented by our repentance and our faithful endurance of the mortal crucible — our own taste of a bitter cup — is a self-sacrifice that mirrors the Savior's own self-sacrifice. He is the Father's, and we are his. The Father is in him, and he is in us. Perhaps in this sense only those whose own sacrificial attitude resembles his, even if only slightly, are prepared to be endowed with his grace.

In this sacrificial spirit, the righteous saints who belong to the Holy One of Israel are those who have endured the crosses of the world and despised the shame of it. These are they who shall inherit the kingdom of God and whose joy shall be full forever.

All of us, like Adam and Eve, must leave God's presence in the quest for knowledge and growth through personal experience. Our exploration will not cease until we return to his presence, prepared at last to grasp, to comprehend—to receive with full understanding of life's meaning—the endowment of a Godlike nature. This sacred gift, the greatest of all the gifts of God, transcends infinitely the limits of man's own power. Knowledge without obedience leads not to a final understanding of life's meaning, but to "sound and fury, signifying nothing."[2] On the other hand, knowledge constrained by obedience to God and then fulfilled by the grace of God leads to meaning, sanctification, and eternal joy.

Nephi taught the relationship between man's experience and God's mercy in a single phrase—it is by grace that we are saved, *after all we can do*. Guided by this perspective, the chapters in "Part I: The Tree of Knowledge" explore some basic characteristics of mortality and the human experience. This exploration will suggest how, through doing "all we can do" in the lone and dreary world, we partake of the *tree of knowledge*.

The chapters in "Part II: The Tree of Life" then consider the nature and role of the Lord's healing and perfecting grace, which the mortal experience prepares us to receive. In its fully flowered form, the *tree of life* gives us both light and life, culminating our eternal quest for knowledge, fulfillment, and understanding; for it is the tree of the life and the light of the world.[3]

Part I

THE TREE OF KNOWLEDGE

CHAPTER ONE

The Life Cycle of Adam and Eve

T he experience of Adam and Eve is an ideal prototype for our own mortal experience. Their story is our story. The complete cycle of their fall from innocence and their ultimate return to God typifies a general human pattern for personal growth that can lead ultimately to deep personal meaning. This perspective will suggest the broad view of "all we can do" along the pathway toward a divine nature.

The lost sheep metaphor derives originally from the Savior's parable: "What man of you, having an hundred sheep, if he lose one of them, doth not leave the ninety and nine in the wilderness, and go after that which is lost, until he find it? And when he hath found it, he layeth it on his shoulders, rejoicing." (Luke 15:4-5.) Ordinarily, when we think of lost sheep, we think of those who become "lost" through deliberate unfaithfulness to God. In our hymn, "Dear to the Heart of the Shepherd," we sing not only of the Shepherd's concern for his sheep, but also of the need for "undershepherds" to help reclaim lost sheep to "the fold," usually meaning activity in the Church. So when we sing, "Out in the desert they wander, hungry and helpless and cold; off to the rescue he hastens," we are normally thinking of those who aren't in church.

I once heard a child tell the parable of the lost sheep in

a way that stirred fresh thoughts about who the lost sheep is. A little girl so tiny that we could barely see the top of her ponytails over the pulpit told the story in a sacrament meeting. Her mother knelt by her side and coached her gently as she talked. She said, "There was once a shepherd who had a hundred sheep. He loved his sheep, so he counted them every day. One day he counted: '. . . ninety-seven, ninety-eight, ninety-nine.' A little sheep was lost. The shepherd went to find him. The little sheep was far off in the rocks and bushes. He was frightened and lonely. The shepherd called, 'Little she-eep . . . ?' The little sheep heard him and was glad. He said, 'Baa-aa.' The shepherd came and found the little sheep. He picked him up and carried him on his shoulder back to his mommy. Then he counted again: '. . . ninety-eight, ninety-nine, one hundred.' All the sheep were safely home."

As I listened, it dawned on me: I am the little lost sheep. Others I know and love — including many who attend church — are the little lost sheep. There are so many times when we feel lost. We can feel lost even if we have not "left the fold" in the sense of leaving the Church or violating major commandments.

Adam and Eve must at times have felt like lost sheep. They were originally in God's presence, then left him through an act we sometimes call a sin, but which might also be called an *act of independence*. They were cast out of their garden of innocence into the lone and dreary world. "Out in the desert they wandered, hungry and helpless and cold." They began to suffer pain as a consequence of their independent action. In humility and childlike faith they called upon God for help. They offered sacrifices as instructed by an angel, even though they had no idea why they should. Through the symbol of sacrifice they were then taught about the Savior and were shown how they could return to God's presence through his Atonement. They rejoiced in the miraculous possibility that he might one day carry them home again into the presence of their father.

What did Adam and Eve know after they returned to God's presence that they hadn't known when they were originally with him in the Garden? What can *we* know after our own return to God that we didn't know in our premortal life? The scriptures explain that God expected and desired that Adam and Eve's children would have the same kinds of mortal experiences as their first parents had, which suggests that the redemption of Adam and Eve was not just a convenient way to erase the effect of an unfortunate error. Rather, it was an intentional element in a course of instruction designed by God himself for their preparation, if they freely chose to accept it. Without that course of instruction, they could not have developed the *capacity* to live a *meaningful* celestial life. So it is with our experience as their children: Mortality is not mere estrangement from God—it is the crucible through which the possibility of truly meaningful life becomes real.

The mortal life cycle of Adam and Eve might be portrayed as the archetype for our own lives.[1] (See chart, page 40.)

In our premortal state we live in "unity with God," the father of our spirits. Through birth into mortality, we begin to experience some distance from him, for we are now subject to death, sin, and a sense of time. Our "acts of independence" may involve sins of deliberate disobedience inspired by Satan, but they also include errors of judgment or choices that do not involve clear-cut, good-versus-evil alternatives. Thus, the "rejection" and "bitterness" we feel reflect the natural consequences of our choices, as well as the guilt feelings that follow sinful action.

The "humility," "reconcilation," and other steps that moved Adam and Eve on around the cycle to eventual reunification with God do not automatically follow for their children. Not all of us learn from the pain caused by our acts of independence. Some leave the path of the natural cycle whenever they feel the approach of psychic pain, straying off course to avoid the discomfort of dealing with unpleasant realities. Others con-

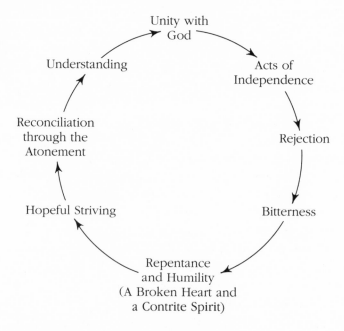

demn themselves so mercilessly that they become immobilized or even drop out at the bottom of the cycle.

But those who respond as Adam and Eve did will learn and grow, moving "after all they can do" through each step in the cycle until they take the outstretched hand of the Atoning One. Thus they cast Satan's influence from their lives and gain both insight and strength as the Savior leads them toward the joy and enlightenment of being reunited with God. The Lord's saving intervention in this cycle is symbolized by the angel who came to Adam to teach him about the Atonement and to explain why he should offer sacrifices. The angel came only after Adam had demonstrated his humble desire to be true and faithful. This pattern is echoed in Abraham's discovery of a ram in the thicket, as discussed toward the end of chapter two.

When we, like Adam and Eve, voluntarily submit to the repentance, humility, and hopeful striving required to begin the homeward turn at the bottom of the cycle (symbolized by a broken heart and a contrite spirit), we will qualify for the full measure of the Savior's atoning power: "Behold he offereth himself a sacrifice for sin, to answer the ends of the law, unto all those who have a broken heart and a contrite spirit; and unto none else can the ends of the law be answered." (2 Nephi 2:7.)

The Atonement adds three crucial elements to our journey that we could not add by ourselves. First, through the law of mercy and on condition of our repentance, the Atonement allows the Savior to pay for our sins committed along the way, thereby satisfying the law of justice and ensuring our personal forgiveness. Without that cleansing power, we could not return to unity with God, because no unclean thing can enter his presence.

Second, subject to our doing "all we can do," the Atonement compensates for the harmful consequences of all our acts of independence, both the consequences we may suffer and the consequences other people suffer through our actions. For example, the resurrection made possible by the Atonement compensates for the physical death all of us will suffer because of Adam and Eve's decisions in the Garden of Eden. This compensation is available not only to redress the effects of sin but also to redress the effects of bitterness resulting from judgment-call choices and undeserved adversity.

Third, the Atonement somehow releases the forces of grace, through which the Savior empowers and endows us with strength, capacity, hope, and other spiritual gifts we may need, both to continue our journey and to reenter God's presence endowed with the requisite attributes.

This developmental cycle portrays human experience at both general and particular levels. As with Adam and Eve, the totality of our experiences can add up to a general pattern of development—the sum of many parts from many years building together toward overall progression. In addition, a large number of specific experiences and developmental stages fit the same cyclical pattern. Indeed, these shorter-range trips around the cycle vividly illustrate the cycle's natural reflection of life. In this "micro" sense, the pattern is more a recurring episode cycle than a single life cycle, but I will use the term *life cycle* for simplicity in referring to both levels of the pattern.

Consider first the example of a baby. For nine months prior to his or her birth, the baby is in literal unity with the mother. But from the moment of birth, the infant child begins a slow but inevitable movement toward independence. At first, he is unaware of his separate existence. He assumes not that he is part of his mother, but that his mother is part of him. His own infant consciousness is for him not only the center of the universe, but all of it. As he begins the mortal journey, he will sense increasingly the difference between his own identity and that of his mother. Ultimately, understanding the reality of his separate status will give significance to his life as he learns of his relationship first to his mother and then to the rest of the universe. In this first mortal experience of self-discovery are the seeds of the idea that the larger life cycle can return us to God's presence with an understanding of who we are, who God is, and what our lives mean. This under-standing is impossible without the experiences that teach us, sometimes painfully, about our own agency and independence. Paradoxically, it is only in discovering our independence from God that we understand our utter dependence on him.

The baby's early movements toward independence can lead to dissonance and frustration as the warm and constant nurturing of unity with his mother is increasingly interrupted. Before long, however, the baby will make the exciting discovery that he is capable of independent action, which introduces both a new sense of power and a new source of frustration. Many of his acts of independence will lead not to the delights of doing as one pleases but to the unhappy surprises of pleasing to do things that bring about disaster—from spilling the milk and touching the stove to eating the dirt and tipping over the tricycle. We call a toddler's life the "terrible twos" primarily because he is suddenly mobile enough to get into things, yet inexperienced enough to keep from getting into all the wrong things. It is a harrowing period for everyone in the family, both for the babies who keep falling and for those who keep trying to catch them before they hit the floor. The toddler reasonably believes his power to walk should take him anywhere, but when every drawer or door will not open, or when those that do open cause his parents to shout at him or grab him, he learns quickly about the pain and alienation that can follow acts of independence.

In trying to help their toddler cope successfully with his growing pains, parents may be tempted to resort to extreme alternatives. One enticing possibility is to confine the child to his bedroom (or even the bed alone) until he is old enough to handle his mobility with less risk of harm. There are times when "old enough" for this purpose seems to be age twenty-five or thirty. But, of course, a child cannot learn at all without *some* experience, so most parents dismiss the total confinement option as unrealistic.

At the other extreme is the temptation to just let the child run free, accompanied by a strong supporting cast of family members who protect him from danger or place desirable objects in his path, whichever way he turns. If he heads for the street in front of the house, someone stops the traffic. If he heads for the drawer containing mommy's makeup or the family cookie supply, someone else quickly replaces the contents with toddler toys. That way, any drawer the child opens contains only pleasant surprises. There would be no tightropes without safety nets. The toddler's environment is thus moved around as if on casters, making his every choice a safe one. This kind of protective permissiveness is motivated by a desire to spare the child pain and frustration. But it, too, is dismissed by most parents, for a child cannot learn in a risk-free environment. Without learning firsthand about natural consequences, a child is never able to live in the natural world. He would remain in a state of innocent helplessness and dependence, having been spared all forms of disappointment.

So most parents lovingly measure out increasing freedom to their toddlers, keeping a watchful eye on them and praying that the inevitable accidents are not terribly serious. Then, when the crash-and-burn moments come along, parents try to help the child learn from his experiences. Successful learning even at this age moves naturally around the life cycle, as parents try to help their children move from bitterness to reconciliation with just enough sense of pain and responsibility that the experience is a real one—but without so much trauma that the child is unwilling to take another step, or unwilling to feel the humility needed to allow a hopeful striving. The more a child experiences the completeness of moving entirely around the cycle, the better he is able to accept successive encounters with natural consequences.

But after a few years, just when we think the child has learned some sense of responsibility and caution, he becomes a teenager. One of the main differences between age two and age sixteen is the size of the risk involved. Because adolescents are bigger and range farther, there is more danger. In other respects the two stages share the basic similarity of a sense of autonomy and power that are frequently unrealistic. It is typical of the adolescent mind to believe he is invincible to the point of being immortal. His inability to anticipate future implications makes him terribly vulnerable to harm from high-risk activities that offer immediate thrills. Automobile insurance rates are higher for teenage drivers for the simple statistical reason that they have far more accidents. They lack the judgmental capacity to evaluate the risk of potential harm, so they drive carelessly.

Research on the problem of cigarette smoking bears out this judgmental limitation in the adolescent perspective. Adults have increasingly responded to warnings about the health risks of smoking. But solemn and persuasive evidence about sharply higher rates of lung cancer among smokers has had a negligible effect among the teenage audience. It is difficult for young people to comprehend the nature of cancer when they lack experience with terminal illnesses. On the other hand, attempts to persuade teens that cigarette smoking is not "cool" have been more successful.

The same kinds of findings appear in research on the use of contraceptives by adolescents. In recent years, contraceptives have become widely available to teenagers because some government planners have believed that increased contraception is the best method to reduce the high American rate of adolescent pregnancies. Some recent research now shows, however, that increased distribution of contraceptives may actually be accompanied by *increases* in adolescent pregnancy rates. This result may well follow from, among other factors, the inability of most adolescents to plan or to anticipate the future well enough to put contraceptives systematically to their intended use, especially in the emotionally charged and value-laden areas of life associated with sexuality. Even if their sexual activity were appropriate, which of course it is not, many teenagers have enough trouble thinking ahead to the next meal or the next day, let alone thinking about consequences nine months into the future.

The story of Icarus in Greek mythology illustrates the carefree and curious attitude toward risk-taking that is so characteristic of the typical adolescent. Icarus and his father, Daedalus, attempted to escape from the island of Crete on homemade wings of wax and feathers. Icarus was thrilled with the excitement of flying for the first time in his life — not unlike the sixteen-year-old taking his first spin at the wheel of a powerful automobile. He wanted to fly higher and higher, but his father cautioned him that if he flew too close to the sun, the heat would melt the wax in his wings and destroy them. Icarus wanted to know how high was too high, for he wanted to fly as close to the edge of disaster as he could get without hurting himself. Not heeding his father, Icarus finally soared higher and higher until the sun did melt the wax in his wings, and he plunged tragically to his death in the sea below. The dilemma for Daedalus, as for other parents, is knowing how to help a child have enough experience to learn from it without allowing, as the saying goes, so much rope that he hangs himself.

I try to keep a clear perspective about the continual experiences my teenage children seem to have with Adam and Eve's life cycle. They need freedom enough to make minor errors so they can learn from their mistakes and discover the connections between decisions and consequences. But they also need protection against the life-threatening hazards of being near-adults in the physical sense while remaining near-children in the developmental sense. A seasoned father once told me, regarding the foibles of adolescent life, that there is a difference between sin and foolishness. His point was that the immature and foolish things teenagers do are not all necessarily sinful. Sometimes they need to experience feelings of foolishness in order to develop an internal sense of proportion strong enough to guide their future decision-making. Such are the experiences that become truly internalized.

The prodigal son — perhaps an adolescent himself — finally found understanding and insight through his foolishness. After he had "wasted his substance with riotous living," he found himself at the bottom of the life cycle, where "he would fain have filled his belly with the husks that the swine did eat: and no man gave unto him." Then, *when he came to himself*," he finally understood that life at his father's home, which he once perceived as inadequate, represented "enough and to spare." He literally ran the rest of the way around the life cycle, with feelings of unworthiness but with a desire to return home, to a life and to parents he had learned to *appreciate* — both in the sense of being grateful and in the sense of comprehending, in part, the kind of life his parents had taught him to live. (Luke 15:11-32.)

It is sometimes possible to learn such lessons by watching the foolishness of others. There is always considerable risk that those who will only learn through their own errors will never return, because there is no assurance that they will learn what is there to be learned. But the point for our common experience with the adolescent stage is the same: Some acts of independence at this time of life are natural and can be the source of significant insight, if only a child's movement around the cycle is complete.

As with the parents of toddlers, the parents of adolescents wonder constantly if they should be more strict or less strict. Either extreme seems to offer a simpler approach — lock them for ten years in their rooms, occasionally slipping a little food under the door; or just turn them loose, shouting after them as they leave the house something like, "You're accountable now for your own sins!" But these years, like the toddler years, are crucial learning years; and for that fundamental purpose, neither extreme discipline nor extreme permissiveness alone will suffice. There must be a combination, weighted this way or that depending on the needs and responsiveness of the individual child, and depending most of all on the disciplinary framework most likely to encourage the process of internalizing the natural principles of life.

Cultural historian Christopher Lasch observed the following about contemporary American family life:

> The best argument for the indispensability of the family is that children grow up best under conditions of intense emotional involvement with their parents. Without struggling with the ambivalent emotions aroused by the union of love and discipline in his parents, the child never masters his inner rage or his fear of authority. It is for this reason that children need parents, not professional nurses or counselors.[2]

Understanding this process of growth is critical to understanding "how the cultural heritage is acquired and internalized by each generation." A child who moves successfully through this application of the life cycle will learn to deal with his father figure (who symbolizes natural laws and, eventually, God) so he can ultimately take a place next to his father (God), rather than making the child feel that he must eliminate or reject his father (God.) Thus a child's growth processes, when discipline and love are appropriately blended by parents, help him "to internalize moral standards in the form of a conscience." Without such an experience, the child never does grow up. "Psychologically he remains in important ways a child, surrounded by authorities with whom he does not identify and whose authority he does not regard as legitimate."[3]

In the life pattern represented in the experience of Adam and Eve, God was the source of both love and discipline. This uniting of love and discipline created a paradox, as did commandments which seemed to urge both their dependence on him and yet their independence from him. In this sense, the relationship of children to their parents is much like our relationship to our Father in Heaven. Our understanding of the desirable process by which children finally untie themselves from parental apron strings, while simultaneously growing in love and appreciation for their parents, helps us understand how God might view us—gently (sometimes not so gently) nourishing both our independence from and our dependence on him.

If children learn the naturalness of Adam and Eve's life cycle from the turmoil of adolescence, they will be better prepared to face their next experiences with the same familiar pattern, such as are found in love and marriage. It is common during and following the adolescent years to develop a great fondness for a person of the opposite sex, only to sense no similar response from the other person. At that point, there may be enough discouragement to bring on what someone has called the "dark night of the soul" at the bottom of the life cycle diagram. Those who hold out their hearts in love only to have them bruised and rejected may feel they will never again allow themselves to fall in love. But the mentally healthy person who perceives the naturalness of the experience will summon the courage to climb back up the cycle toward greater reconciliation with the opposite sex in general. This person will learn lessons for the future from the experience, both about himself and about the way relationships develop. Others will have a harder time, wrongly equating rejection by one person with rejection by everyone. Instead of learning from the experience, some will develop bitter feelings or lose their self-confidence, as potential movements around the cycle do not materialize into productive opportunities.

The universality of the life cycle is also found in marriage. When two people come together from unique backgrounds, there will inevitably be times of misunderstanding or differences in perspective. Such times may suddenly create a sense of distance between partners who have in fact been moving closer together. The difference between a successful and an unsuccessful marriage is not in whether there are such times of tension, but in whether and how the tensions are resolved.

In today's society, an increasing number of people seem to assume that happiness and fulfillment are threatened by relationships and commitments that tie them down. As a result, many who experience marital differences elect to leave the scene of the conflict by either literally or figuratively divorcing themselves from the person they view as the source of their frustrations. Many of these in time will marry another person, only to find another set of conflicts and frustrations. Then they will again leave what they believe is the source of the conflict, the relationship, somehow believing they are entitled to live without the inconvenience and stress of dealing with points of view different from their own. Often their cry will be, "I'm entitled to a little happiness." If so, they do not realize that happiness is found through the maturing of a relationship based on commitment and self-sacrifice, not by running away from the demanding experiences that give meaning to a relationship.

Those who in this sense veer away from the demanding course of the life cycle at the first sign of pain or bitterness may never experience the humility, the soul-searching, the sensitive reaching out, and the reconciliation that come in finally understanding things from the perspective of another person, or in subordinating one's own needs to those of another. By missing these natural, though at times painful, steps, common to those who live in the enduring bonds of honest marital love, they deprive themselves of the experiences necessary to fully discover love and joy.

On the other hand, those who remain committed enough that leaving is not an alternative are likely to make remarkable discoveries about their spouses and about themselves. Significantly, these discoveries may have profound effects upon their own personal maturation and development. In this way, the overall life cycle of a good marriage, made up of multiple experiences moving through all the levels of developmental growth suggested by the life cycle of Adam and Eve, will usually bear the sweet and mellow fruit of mature personal character.

By using such commonplace examples as children and marriage, I have hoped to suggest the universal nature of the life cycle. In addition to, or perhaps as the composite effect of, these smaller-scale developmental experiences, our lives in a more general sense may resemble the Adamic pattern. We will have our times of feeling cast out of our gardens of closeness to God into the lone and dreary world. But there we also learn to distinguish good from evil by our own experience. There we encounter the thorns and weeds among which life's precious fruits are found. Without some knowledge of thorns, the very preciousness of the fruit would be lost on us.

We also earn our bread in the sweat of our faces; and in suffering we bring forth children, with some of us facing similar tragic losses in our children's lives as Adam and Eve experienced when they "lost" *both* Abel and Cain. And we, too, will sense the joy of our redemption, as did Eve, when the Good Shepherd who cared for her also carries us home on his shoulder. The story of Adam and Eve is our story.

CHAPTER TWO

Entering the
Life Cycle

W hen we talk of the Atonement and our need for the Savior's help, we often assume that we enter Adam and Eve's life cycle primarily—even exclusively—by acts of sin. Frequently the same assumption is made about the entry of Adam himself into the cycle. In fact, however, we, like Adam and Eve, may enter the cycle in a variety of ways. That is why the term *acts of independence* is a more broadly descriptive phrase than *sin* as the first step in the cycle. That is also why I have used examples from everyday human experience with babies, adolescents, and marriage to demonstrate that the acts that launch us along this path are not always "sinful." Once we understand that many of life's natural experiences lead us along sorrowful paths, we will be less likely to assume that only willful sinners may feel pain and estrangement from God. We are also less likely to be surprised when we discover that even the straight and narrow path—the path we ought to be treading—is not a trouble-free high road, for it is the same path trod by Adam and Eve.

Consider three different ways of entering the life cycle: sin, errors of judgment, and adversity.

The first and most obvious act of independence from God is deliberate sin. Those who sow the seeds of sin will reap, and often force others to reap, the consequences of their defiant acts. There is a kind of harmonic ecology in the laws of nature which, when violated, reflects an ecological disturbance. With some sins, the consequences can be devastating and immediate, such as with acts of violence against other people or physical abuse to one's own body. With other sins, such as with certain forms of immorality, the negative results may manifest themselves more slowly. Often, the less tangible transgressions will more completely canker the soul, perhaps because they have longer to spread their internally destructive force before their corrosion surfaces enough that it must be faced.

The story of Alma the Younger provides a striking illustration of both the internal effects of sin and the way the second and upward half of the life cycle brings recompense. (See Alma 36.) Alma and the sons of Mosiah had gone about intentionally "seeking to destroy the church" of God, until an angel stopped them in a dramatic manifestation. (See Mosiah 27.) Alma was unable to speak or move for three days. During this time, he descended to the bottom of the life cycle. He felt alienated from God to the point of fearing his own destruction. As he began remembering his sins in detail, his soul was so "tormented with the pains of hell" that "the very thought of coming into the presence of . . . God did rack [his] soul with inexpressible horror." He wanted to cease existing. Then, while thus plunged into his dark night of the soul, he *remembered the teachings of his father concerning the coming of Christ.* Responding in deep and repentant humility, Alma cried, "O Jesus, thou Son of God, have mercy on me." (See Alma 36:13, 14, 18.) As the forgiveness process began, he sensed a sweet and exquisite joy.

During this experience Alma believed he glimpsed God's presence, and his "soul did long to be there." (Alma 36:22.) With the infusion of strength from such a hope, he took the healing hand of the Atoning One, who lifted him up to begin a new course of life. He knew his reconciliation with God was under way: "The knowledge which I have is of God." (Alma 36:26.) In a spirit of true restitution, he "labored without ceasing" to bring other souls to repentance, experiencing along the way the constant support of God "under trials and troubles of every kind." Thus did he understand and appreciate the "everlasting power" of God. Each step around the life cycle, including both the compensating and the life-giving roles of the Atonement, is vividly represented in Alma's experience.

Among its other lessons, Alma's story bears witness to the power of parental teachings to return in a child's memory at some critical, future time — even though a child may appear to pay little attention at all when the teaching first occurs. The story of Enos bears a second witness to this truth. As he "went to hunt beasts in the forests" by himself, "the words which [he] had often heard [his] father speak concerning eternal life, and the joy of the saints, sunk deep into [his] heart." (Enos 1:2, 3.) We don't know, of course, how much time elapsed between the teaching and the eventual learning in the cases of Alma and Enos, but in the long run that may not matter much. Parents whose children seem to ignore their teachings in the present should never give up, for the seeds they plant may lie dormant for many seasons before they suddenly and powerfully take root.

Not everyone who follows Alma into this classic pathway is willing to take each step as it comes. Some try to short-circuit the process of repentance when they first sense the approaching pain. Some even veer entirely off the circular path to avoid that confining discomfort, never to return to the cycle at all. Others may become stuck at the bottom of the cycle in the despair of lost hope. Still others stay within the cycle but instinctively seek a shortcut, dashing across the middle of the circle shown in the life cycle diagram from "rejection" to "reconciliation" without enduring the bitterness, humility, repentance and hopeful striving experienced by Alma — both in his moment of recognition and in his subsequent life.

But there is more to the process of genuine repentance than merely preferring acceptance by God to the initial feeling of estrangement from him. That process requires us to endure the full fury of sin's bitterness, the shame that may accompany confession, and the honest humility of facing up to our own unworthiness. If we prefer to "hurry and repent" merely by switching our declared allegiance from evil to good in some quick moment of verbal acknowledgment, we will circumvent the painful but life-altering experiences that would otherwise allow us to emerge from a sinful experience stronger than when we entered it.

A second way of entering the life cycle is by making mistakes or errors of judgment. Some of these actions might also be called sins committed in ignorance. For example, we might act selfishly or insensitively in family relationships, or allow self-interest to cloud our view of another person's needs. There is usually a difference between errors of this nature and serious sin, just as there is a difference among teenagers between foolishness and sin. The law also distinguishes between intentional wrongdoing and carelessness or negligence. Criminal acts, for instance, require proof of conscious criminal intent, suggesting that our moral culpability is higher with deliberate sin than it is with foolish errors. Regardless of our intentions, however, our careless decisions can lead to consequences that harm others as seriously as would a willful decision to hurt them.

Shakespeare's tragedy *King Lear* illustrates how poor judgment can lead a person into the life cycle of Adam and Eve. At the beginning of the story, King Lear announces that he is ready to divide his kingdom among his three daughters. But first he wishes to hear each one express her love for him in the presence of his court. Cordelia, the only honest daughter of the three, is shocked and hurt by this procedure. She has sincerely demonstrated her love for Lear throughout her life, and believes she should "love, and be silent." In an aside to the audience, Cordelia explains, "Unhappy that I am, I cannot heave my heart into my mouth." After her two sisters have superficially declared their love for Lear in flowery terms, Cordelia has nothing to say. She cannot cheapen her love with a few easy words. The king is embarrassed, but she will not yield. In frustration and anger, he banishes Cordelia and divides the kingdom between the other two daughters. Cordelia marries the king of France and leaves the country.

Lear then learns from sad experience that the daughters who gave the lovely speeches have no real love for him. They turn him out of their houses, and he enters upon his own dark night of the soul. His earlier act of poor judgment now casts him literally and figuratively into the lone and dreary world, symbolized vividly by a famous scene that shows him staggering through a fierce storm, rejected by his own children, and trying to make sense of his life as all nature seems to rage against him.

Finally Cordelia finds Lear in the midst of his maddening agony. In a tender reconciliation scene, the king acknowledges his error. But Cordelia, perhaps a Christ figure who lifts Lear up from the bottom of the cycle toward redemption and atonement, honors him with her constant love and respect. She then boldly accompanies Lear as they seek by military force to regain his throne from the other daughters and their husbands. In the process, Cordelia loses her life, offering the ultimate sacrifice in her devotion to her father. As the tragic play ends, Lear holds Cordelia in his arms, informed by a new understanding of love through the witness of both her life and her death. Lear, like Alma, moved all the way around the circle of experience, learning, finally, but at great cost. As Shakespeare elsewhere put it:

> And ruin'd love when it is built anew
> Grows fairer than at first, more strong, far greater.
> So I return rebuk'd to my content,
> And gain by ills thrice more than I have spent.
> (Sonnet 119.)

There is yet a third way of entering the life cycle of Adam and Eve, a way brought about not by our wrongful or careless choices, but by the very nature of mortality. Adversity seems to stalk us as an ever present potential companion, regardless of our worthiness. In the midst of these afflictions, especially because they seem totally undeserved and unnecessary, our need for the compensating power and the affirmative endowments made possible by the Atonement may be more acute than at any other time of life.

Even the most faithful among us will have moments of loneliness and rejection. From Liberty Jail, Joseph Smith cried out, "O God, where art thou? And where is the pavilion that covereth thy hiding place?" (D&C 121:1.) Soon afterward, the voice of the Spirit whispered to Joseph: "Know thou, my son, that all these things shall give thee experience, and shall be for thy good. The Son of Man hath descended below them all. Art thou greater than he?" (D&C 122:7-8.) Jeremiah had a similar struggle: "O Lord, . . . thou art stronger than I, and hast prevailed. . . . Then I said, I will not make mention of him, nor speak any more in his name. But his word was in mine heart as a burning fire shut up in my bones. . . . But the Lord is with me as a mighty terrible one." (Jeremiah 20:7-9, 11.) And even the Savior, in his hour of greatest darkness and greatest triumph, pleaded, "If thou be willing, remove this cup from me: nevertheless not my will, but thine, be done." (Luke 22:42.)

The Old Testament prophet Elijah tasted of the life cycle during his heroic efforts to fulfill his prophetic calling. In the depth of his discouragement "he requested for himself that he might die; and said, It is enough; now, O Lord, take away my life; for I am not better than my fathers." (1 Kings 19:4.) Elijah's climb from this dark night of the soul is depicted in Mendelssohn's oratorio *Elijah*, which contains an exquisite musical representation of the Lord stretching forth his hand of atonement to aid his faithful prophet in distress. While asleep under a juniper tree in exhausted depression, Elijah is visited by angels, who sing with great reassurance, "Lift thine eyes to the mountains, whence cometh help," followed by, "He, watching over Israel, slumbers not, nor sleeps." Then an angel sings to Elijah that sublime song of assurance, "O rest in the Lord;

wait patiently for Him, and He shall give thee thy heart's desires."

Strengthened by this support from beyond the veil, Elijah arises and is led to Horeb, the mount of God, where the Lord reassures him in a powerful but intimate exchange. Following a great wind, an earthquake, and a fire, comes "a still small voice," the voice of the Lord, strengthening Elijah and sending him back on his prophetic way. He returns to warn the people, singing a text drawn from Isaiah: "For the mountains shall depart, and the hills be removed; but Thy kindness shall not depart from me, neither shall the covenant of Thy peace be removed."

Throughout much of Old Testament history, Jehovah was thought to be a jealous God whose protection depended upon the obedience of his people. If the people were faithful, they felt assured of his protection against any adverse force. Therefore, when trouble came it was natural to assume that the cause was personal unrighteousness, either for an individual or for Israel as a nation. But the story of Job reveals important insights about God and adversity. Job's experience demonstrates that we can enter Adam and Eve's life cycle not only because of our transgressions, and not only because of our unwise choices, but because adversity is a natural — even an important — part of life: "Man that is born of a woman is of few days, and full of trouble. . . . His flesh upon him shall have pain, and his soul within him shall mourn." (Job 14:1, 22.) Yet Job's friends took for granted the traditional assumption that wickedness was the only possible explanation for his afflictions and, correspondingly, that obedience would assure his prosperity: "If thou return to the Almighty, thou shalt be built up. . . . Yea, the Almighty shall be thy defence, and thou shalt have plenty of silver." (Job 22:23, 25.) His wife was more willing to accept the assumption made by the gentiles that when trouble comes to Jehovah's followers, it must be because he is not powerful enough to protect them. "Dost thou still retain thine integrity? curse God, and die." (Job 2:9.) Only Job sensed, even though he could not fully understand, that he could and should trust God enough to move on around the cycle, for his sorrows signified neither God's weakness nor Job's unworthiness. "Though he slay me, yet will I trust in him." (Job 13:15.)

It is not always clear whether one's entry into the pattern of the life cycle is the result of sin, errors of judgment, adversity, or some other circumstance. Adam's own case is ambiguous enough to make that point. But whatever the explanation (if we can find it at all) for our entry into the natural bitterness of mortality, the very universality of such an experience may be the most important thing to understand. In seeing that broad vision, we may expand ourselves enough to learn lessons of enormous significance and meaning from our difficult experiences.

There may even be a fundamental religious necessity in the universal opportunity we have for experiences that take our own souls into some dark night. Joseph Smith taught that "a religion that does not *require* the sacrifice of all things never has power sufficient to produce the faith necessary unto life and salvation."[1] Abraham, that archetype of the principle of sacrifice, was asked to sacrifice Isaac, his child of promise, under circumstances at least as irrational as those Job faced. In Abraham's case, he was asked to be the instrumentality of his own affliction, by performing the sacrifice himself. This alone placed God's request of Abraham beyond human ability to understand. In addition, to sacrifice Isaac was to destroy in one stroke all hope of fulfilling God's glorious promise that through the son of Abraham and Sarah the everlasting covenant would continue. Thus the image of Abraham standing over Isaac on the altar with a raised knife represents the ultimate leap of religious faith. There he stood, simultaneously at the height of faithful obedience and at the depth of personal anguish.

Then, by pure grace — in this instance through a ram in the thicket — God released Abraham from His awful commandment. In this striking symbol of the Atonement, God led Abraham into his soul's dark night, then transformed the experience into a moment of light. Abraham's willingness to give more than his own life made him worthy to receive the additional promise that through his seed all nations of the earth would be blessed, meaning the birth of Christ. Thus did "the father of faith" make his own way around the life cycle, accepting the Lord's sacrifice by virtue of his own willingness to sacrifice everything, thus reinforcing Adam's pattern of sacrifice for his posterity. Abraham also entered the cycle not through his own wrongdoing or misjudgment, nor even through nature's adversities, but through the express invitation of God.

Whether we descend into the dark night of our own soul through transgression, unwise choices, natural opposition, the invitation of God, or some mixture of causes, the crucial issue is whether we can in that experience yield our broken hearts contritely to God. This willingness to sacrifice all things must reach broadly and deeply enough to include the sacrifice of our sins, our vanity, our self-esteem, and our love for worldly comforts. Sometimes we must also sacrifice our determination to understand to our rational satisfaction *why* we should be lost in the darkness. When the light of the Savior's atoning power finally pierces that darkness, compensating for our bitterness and carrying us on up the cycle to reconciliation and reunity with God, the blessing of understanding will finally be ours, one result of "arriving where we started and knowing the place for the first time."[2]

Remember once more the parable of the lost sheep. I was once in a gospel doctrine class in which we discussed the many scriptural references to sheep and lambs. We read the Savior's words: "I am the good shepherd: the good shepherd giveth his life for the sheep." (John 10:11.) "Doth he not leave the ninety and nine, and goeth into the mountains, and seeketh that which is gone astray?" (Matthew 18:12.) At the end of the class, a woman I knew well was asked to say the closing prayer. She was a kind and faithful woman who lived with the daily agony of caring for her elderly husband, who was a victim of a debilitating disease. He was completely and permanently disoriented and unable to care for himself. Those who must care for loved ones in such a condition carry burdens that outsiders can never understand. In her prayer, this woman expressed gratitude for the gospel, the Church, and the relationships among our class members. She prayed for the lost sheep who need the gospel but do not accept it. Then she said with both courage and humility, "And help us, too, Father, when we sometimes are lost."

Her words caused me to think of another older woman who has experienced much sorrow in her life. After losing several close family members in death, she developed a painful illness that required surgery. It was to be a risky operation, involving vital nerves and organs. She knew of the risks and worried about them. The night before entering the hospital, she asked for a priesthood blessing, saying, "I am afraid. I want to know that everything will be all right."

The lost sheep are not just the people who don't come to church. The lost sheep are those two good and loyal women. The lost sheep is a mother who goes down into the valley of the dark shadows to bring forth children. The lost sheep is a young person, far away from home and faced with loneliness and temptation. The lost sheep is a person who has just lost a critically needed job; a business person in financial distress; a new missionary in a foreign culture; a man just called to be bishop; a married couple who are misunderstanding each other; a grandmother whose children are forgetting her. I am the lost sheep. You are the lost sheep. "*All* we like sheep have gone astray." (Isaiah 53:6; emphasis added.)

The times of feeling lost are not always times when we have wandered from the straight and narrow path. Not at all. We may be precisely where the Lord would have us be.

Now we may find richer meaning in a little girl's story about a lost sheep. "There was once a shepherd who had a hundred sheep. He thought some of them were lost and so he counted: ' . . . ninety-seven, ninety-eight, ninety-nine.' A little sheep was lost. Far off in the rocks and bushes was the little sheep. He was frightened and lonely. The shepherd went to find him: 'Little she-eep . . . ?' The little sheep heard him and was glad. The shepherd came and picked him up. He carried him on his shoulder back to his mommy. Then he counted again: ' . . . ninety-eight, ninety-nine, one hundred.' All the sheep were safely home."

Consider the lines from Harry Rowe Shelley's "The King of Love my Shepherd Is":

> *The king of love my shepherd is*
> *Whose goodness faileth never.*
> *I nothing lack if I am his*
> *And he is mine forever.*
>
> *Perverse and foolish oft I strayed,*
> *But yet in love he sought me.*
> *And on his shoulder gently laid*
> *And home rejoicing brought me.*

We may stray through sin, we may stray through being "perverse and foolish," or we may be blown astray by the stiff winds of adversity. Whatever the source of our wandering, we are likely to have our own deep experience with Adam and Eve's life cycle, leaving God's presence for the lone and dreary world with the hope of returning to him when someday we are ready. If we in that dark tunnel do all *we* can, we will see at the tunnel's end the light of him who forgives, sweetens, and makes recompense for all our troubles. When we do return, offering our broken heart to him whose broken heart binds up our own, we will understand life in ways we could not have understood before leaving. We will then be conscious of the difference between our Father's identity and ours, conscious of our independence, conscious of our dependence. Then we will *understand* what it means to say, "I am his" and "he is mine forever."

CHAPTER THREE

Opposition and Joy

T he ultimate purpose of the Atonement is to ensure our happiness and joy. But the Lord achieves that purpose in our lives through the interaction of conflicting forces that, at first, seem determined to rob us of the joy we seek. Paradoxically, our purest joy emerges from the natural tension between those opposing forces.

Father Lehi taught his son Jacob that "to answer the ends of the atonement" God has affixed "punishment" and "happiness" in "opposition" to each other as alternative consequences for "the ends of the law which the Holy One hath given." (2 Nephi 2:10.) This same opposition is reflected in the relationship between the two trees in the Garden of Eden: "even the forbidden fruit in opposition to the tree of life; the one being sweet and the other bitter." (2 Nephi 2:15.) We find such opposition everywhere, for "it *must* needs be, that there is an opposition *in all things*." (2 Nephi 2:11; emphasis added.)

Lehi's teachings on this subject emphasize the need for choice and agency, but they also illuminate the way in which opposing forces combine to give meaning to righteous choices. Without the taste of bitter in our experience, the taste of sweet is lost on us—we are without context, without a frame of reference, and even the sweet things of life may be without meaning or purpose for us. Thus, Adam and Eve needed to experience the "misery" of mortality in order to comprehend the sweet taste of joy. If they had remained in Eden, "they would have remained in a state of innocence, *having no joy, for they knew no misery; doing no good, for they knew no sin.*" (2 Nephi 2:23; emphasis added.)

Perhaps because of the way this grand paradox gives perspective to the bitter moments in our daily experience, Lehi introduced his topic by referring to Jacob's brothers' "rudeness" toward him. Then he said, "Nevertheless, Jacob, . . . thou knowest the greatness of God; and *he shall consecrate thine afflictions for thy gain.*" (2 Nephi 2:2; emphasis added.) And after he spoke to Jacob, Lehi shared a poignant, personal example of this theme—a father's tender joy in his small, last-born son, who was "born in the wilderness of . . . afflictions; yea, in the days of . . . greatest sorrow." (2 Nephi 3:1.)[1]

Lehi's reference to the "rudeness" of Jacob's brothers suggests a specific form of "opposition" that is more sharply focused than our typical approaches to the subject of adversity. To be "afflicted" by the "rudeness" of others does not suggest a major tragedy. Rather, it suggests those minor, never-ending afflictions in which we are likely to discover the naturalness— and, hence, the meaning—of opposition in all things.

Opposition of this kind can show up when we least expect it—such as when we think we have just finished with it. For example, many students who enroll at LDS Church-owned universities and colleges are caught off guard when they discover opposition in what they believed would be a trouble-free environment. "Christianity without tears" is what Aldous Huxley called the state some students hope for. One manifestation of this pattern begins when students must work their way through considerable opposition in order to qualify themselves to be admitted to a Church-owned institution. It is not uncommon for LDS young people to experience traumatic "withdrawal" symptoms as they cut their ties with high school friends (both members and nonmembers of the Church) who are not sympathetic to the idea of going to a place such as Ricks College or BYU—which to some friends seems all too much like entering a monastery or a convent.

Sometimes these young people are truly heroic in making the life-style changes they need. I have great admiration for those who walk away from the dazzling lure of worldly friends and enticements and then make deeply felt promises to parents, bishops, and to their Father in Heaven. They often come to these campuses on the wings of new life, bringing a momentum and a determination that results in permanent changes for the better, not only in their own lives, but also in the lives of their roommates and classmates.

But frequently, just when they believe they've left their opposition behind—as if they had launched their rocket ships all the way through the backward pull of gravity—these students discover that opposition has stowed away on board, for it crawls out of the closet when they have hardly unpacked their bags. There may be unstable roommates who have not yet made a genuine break from their habits of the past; there may be disappointments with what appeared to be ideal arrangements for housing or classes; or, surprisingly, there may be new forms of temptation to which the unsuspecting are especially vulnerable when they let down their normal guard. Some have the mistaken impression that when another LDS student wants them to do something questionable, it must be all right because they're all back in the Garden of Eden, having forsaken the lone and dreary world. But if our Church campuses are the Garden of Eden, they unfortunately still have their share of serpents.

Sometimes the problems students face are more mundane, but they can still be discouraging and surprising for those who attend a Church college to escape opposition, not to find more of it. (But that is precisely the point: opposition is in all things, so we may find it in its most interesting forms exactly when we think we have just overcome enough opposition to leave it all behind.) One fall evening during my term as president of Ricks College, I received a phone call from a student's father.

He was calling to complain about a problem his daughter had encountered in trying to register for her classes with our new computerized registration system. I explained that our system was new and might still have a few "bugs" in it, but said we would do all we could to solve her problem. Then he said, clearly frustrated, "Well, I might have expected computer foul-ups at another college, but Ricks is a Church school!" I replied that we must buy our computers at the same place as anyone else. He was not greatly comforted.

New converts may also be vulnerable to unexpected opposition. Having overcome many forms of resistance to reach the point of baptism and having at last found the true church (whose members are even called "saints"), they can experience disillusionment when they discover the imperfections in other Church members.

I once read the brief journal of a young man who joined the Church in Switzerland in the late 1800s. After sensing the enthusiasm of his fellow Latter-day Saints about gathering to Zion, he jumped at the chance to accept the invitation of a Church member in Utah who was looking for a young man to help on his farm. He joined a small company of Swiss immigrants headed for Utah, leaving his family in his green and fertile homeland, promising to make all needed arrangements for their eventual move to the promised new land. After a long, long journey by ship and by train, he had a mixup in meeting his host in Ogden, but finally made other arrangements, traveling two days by horse and buggy to the host's farm. When he arrived at his new home, the young man, fresh from the lush greenery of Switzerland, wonderingly examined the parched and sparsely vegetated desert. He looked around at the humble pioneer cabins and then asked in utter disbelief, "Is *this* Zion?"[2]

In time he came to understand the words of his host: "Yes, here we are building Zion." But until then, he grappled with the shock of facing unexpected opposition, for he thought he had overcome his only real opposition just to get there.

Eliza R. Snow addressed the lines of a pioneer hymn to those who were coming to Zion in the belief that they had left all the afflictions of the world behind them. Her words are also appropriate for new students at a Church school, or for those entering a new marriage, a new location, or almost any other highly promising new experience. (The song's title, "Think Not, When You Gather to Zion," aptly describes the vain hope of some new students at Church schools, who come expecting somehow that they won't have to study quite as hard as might be required elsewhere.)

> *Think not when you gather to Zion*
> *Your troubles and trials are through,*
> *That nothing but comfort and pleasure*
> *Are waiting in Zion for you.*
> *Think not when you gather to Zion,*
> *That all will be holy and pure;*
> *That fraud and deception are banished,*
> *And confidence wholly secure.*
>
> *Think not when you gather to Zion,*
> *The prize and the victory won.*
> *Think not that the warfare is ended,*
> *The work of salvation is done.*
> *No, no; for the great prince of darkness*
> *A tenfold exertion will make,*
> *When he sees you go to the fountain,*
> *Where freely the truth you may take.*

There is opposition in Zion, or at a Church college, because there is opposition in all things. A great deal of significant learning, about spiritual and personal matters as well as matters of the intellect, comes from working through stressful, frustrating opposition. If that is true, then coming to a serious place of learning (such as a college) really *ought* to bring us in contact with potentially productive opposition.

Opposition may take us by surprise in other experiences made memorable partly by their implied promise of better times ahead. Consider the example of marriage. Many young people assume if they can just get married, all their problems will be solved. One new bride reportedly said to her mother on her wedding day, "Oh, Mom, I'm so happy! I'm at the end of my troubles." "Yes, dear," replied the wise mother, "but which end?"

I think of a young couple standing on a soggy lawn at the Idaho Falls Temple one beautiful spring day to have their pictures taken following their temple marriage. It was a picturesque scene, until the groom inadvertently stepped on the ruffled hem of the bride's white gown, mashing it into the wet, muddy grass. She gently asked him to move his foot, but he was too happy to hear her. She needed to speak with more intensity and both were embarrassed. Then they had little choice but to stand through the reception a short time later, hoping to conceal the smudge that suggested, symbolically, that even a temple marriage has its share of opposition—from the beginning.

My wife, Marie, once recalled her own experience with the surprise of finding opposition in becoming married and having her first baby:

> I remember our June wedding day as such a happy occasion. I think of our first summer, when we both worked at Jackson Lake Lodge in Wyoming, in the shadows of those majestic Teton mountains on whose tops we felt we were sitting—because we, as most newlyweds do, felt on top of the world. My memory is happily quite selective about the parts it leaves out—like the fact that my husband was sick much of the summer, or the fact that our lives were turned upside down by the unexpected death of his father a few months after our marriage. Or I think of our experiences with the question of when to start our family. It was only after much soul searching, fasting, prayer, and reading the statements of Church leaders, that we decided we really should not wait to begin having children. After overcoming

considerable opposition in making that decision, we then — to our great surprise — began to discover what Lehi was talking about when he said that if Adam and Eve had remained in the Garden and had had no children, "they would have remained in a state of innocence, having no joy, for they knew no misery." (2 Nephi 2:23.) That scripture seems to say, if they had had no children, they would have known no misery. Only the parents of two-year-olds and teenagers can understand that. But notice — it also says that without children and misery they would have had no joy. How important is joy? Within two verses, Lehi tells us "men *are,* that they might have [that very] joy." (2 Nephi 2:25.)

In my case, here is what all that meant in a down-to-earth sense. After making the great leap of faith involved in deciding to have our first child whenever Mother Nature wanted to send him or her, how was the joyful news of pregnancy made manifest? I was sick. Odd way to be showered with "joy." For part of each day for several months, I felt one degree of terrible or another. It was morning sickness "ad nauseum." Then about four weeks before delivery, I threatened to miscarry, so I spent a number of days in bed, which seriously complicated the classes I was both taking and teaching. But when the big day finally came, even the hours of labor were worth it, as I lay there in my hospital bed holding that beautiful little boy in my arms, his reddish hair already hinting at his temperament. I thought, "Nothing could be more wonderful than this. Surely the world stops for such a beautiful baby." I can remember being shocked when I heard that another mother had another baby just minutes after I had had ours. It seemed our experience had been unique, nonrepeatable. The day after the baby was born, I was cuddling him happily in my hospital room when my doctor came in. He was my uncle and quite a salty character. He looked at us and said cheerily, "How does it feel to have the easiest part over with?" "Easiest part?" I asked. "Why, sure," he replied. "It's the next twenty years that are going to be tough."

Now, almost exactly twenty years later, I understand. After all the diapers, the bruises, the washing, the cheering, the cleaning up, the pleading, the nail-biting, the crying, the laughing, the pacing, and the praying, I understand. I feel about raising children the way Ammon felt about missionary work. "And this is the account of Ammon and his brethren, their journeyings in the land of Nephi, *their sufferings in the land, their sorrows, and their afflictions, and their incomprehensible joy.*" (Alma 28:8.)[3]

There is Lehi's paradox: "He shall consecrate thine afflictions for thy gain." There *is* a link between sorrow, toil, affliction, and "incomprehensible joy." Otherwise, there may only be innocence—"having no joy, for they knew no misery." (2 Nephi 2:23.)

Missionary work is, like marriage, a natural place to find unexpected but potent opposition. The opposition usually begins in the decision to go. A young man who was struggling to decide between marriage and a mission said to his teacher, "I'm not sure she wants me to go. I can't stand to take the chance of losing her. What if we decide to get married instead?" Then he felt a prophet's solemn words reverberate and echo between his ears and in his heart: "Every worthy young man should fulfill a mission. Every worthy young man . . . ." Eventually this young man overcame the opposition and left to serve a mission. I admire the faith of young sweethearts who decide to trust the Lord in that way. It is not easy for them. But even when they find the courage to go, that, like having the baby, may be the easy part.

The Missionary Training Center is a real surprise for missionaries who have never had the experience of sustained intellectual effort. They are likely to work harder, with more intensity and longer hours, than they've ever worked in their lives. They learn firsthand about opposition in the learning process, even while pursuing a righteous path. Yet the success rate and the achievement levels among missionaries in the MTC are truly miraculous. Missionaries are typically on a well-earned "high" as they leave for their fields of labor all over the world. But opposition comes right along to the airport and the rest of the journey. There is opposition in all good things, not just in bad things.

During my own missionary days in Germany, I discovered the mission-field version of opposition — we had our share of rainstorms, dogs, sad news from home, feisty ministers, concerned relatives, and problem missionaries. But few things hurt as much as losing a good investigator — they were so rare. Once, after weeks of fruitless, frustrating tracting in a new city, we found a golden family. They were a handsome young couple with two small children. How well they had received the first three lessons. How warm they were each time we came to see them. What a contribution we knew they would make to the struggling little branch. They seemed destined to become an ideal Latter-day Saint family.

The night the fourth discussion was scheduled, we went bouncing up the stairs to the front door. Our anticipation of this evening had sustained us through days of discouragement. We rang the bell cheerfully. There was no answer. We rang again. Still no answer. We knocked. How strange it seemed. The lights in the house were on when we arrived. We stepped back from the house, threw a little pebble at a lighted upstairs window, and called, "It's us, the missionaries. We're here for the appointment!" The light upstairs went out. Then the other lights went out. All was dark and silent. In shocked disbelief, we looked at each other and then began to cry. As we trudged back to our bicycles, I felt real pain in my heart. "How can they do this to us?" I said to my companion, choking back the tears. He added, "How can they do this to themselves?" It was one of those sad and lonely missionary nights when all the pep talks about having a positive mental attitude fade away like so much salesman's chatter. At such quiet times missionaries can face stiff opposition, feeling unloved, unneeded, and personally rejected.

But disappointments of this kind only sharpened my appreciation for those rare moments when we did see a few wonderful people not only join the Church but partake fully of its blessings over time. Not long ago, just such a family and two of their five children were in our home. They had come from Germany to pick up their son, who had just completed a mission in northern Utah. Their oldest daughter had served a mission in northern Germany, the mother has been a Relief Society president, and the father has been a bishop. We enjoyed a long, refreshing visit, sharing our memories of their conversion experience. We talked about our children and our experiences in the Church. I was stirred deeply by realizing what the gospel can mean to good people after they have enjoyed its long-term fruits and blessings over a generation of time. As we shook hands when they left for home, our eyes met, and the *meaning* of our experiences together flooded my heart with sweet feelings. The words of the Lord's promise echoed through my mind. After the disappointments and frustrations of my missionary experience, enough time had passed to bring a ripening perspective, and I was beginning to understand that "if it so be that you should labor all your days in crying repentance . . . and bring, save it be one soul unto me, how great shall be your joy with him in the kingdom of my Father!" (D&C 18:15.)

Another area in which we sometimes experience natural opposition is the development of testimony. It is not uncommon for new investigators or new converts to be surprised by the patience and the effort required to nurture the seeds of testimony. Actually, most of the questions we face as our testimonies grow are signs that we are learning more, not less, about the truth. I once heard Elder Theodore M. Burton explain that when we first realize we have a testimony, the amount of spiritual truth we know could be symbolized by drawing and coloring in a tiny circle about the size of a pinhead. As our understanding progresses, the circle grows. When our knowledge develops to a certain point of maturity, the circle may be the size of a coin — many times bigger than our first little pinhead of knowledge. When we compare those two colored circles on a piece of paper, the tiny testimony and the larger testimony are surrounded by large areas of white, representing the unknown. As our knowledge grows in relation to the unknown, something unexpected happens. In the larger circle, the much longer circumference around the edge of the circle now puts the testimony in much greater contact with the unknown. Thus, there are many new points at which questions can arise. The more we know, the more potential opposition we face. But it is through the "growing pains" of dealing with that opposition that our knowledge and understanding increase geometrically.

Based on his extended study of the subject, a college student began having some questions about Church history. The more he studied, the more he learned; yet, because historical records are inherently incomplete, he also kept finding new questions to which there were inadequate answers. Because he was unable to find a complete answer to every question that came up, he became very frustrated. He began thinking that if he couldn't solve every historical puzzle he found, perhaps he was violating his integrity to remain active in the Church. At the same time, he loved the Church and had had a sacred experience on his mission that gave him a deep and enduring faith in the reality of Jesus Christ.

After months of struggling, he decided to put aside his unresolved questions and exercise his faith. He would simply have a believing heart. His faith began to grow again, not so much from new information as from new experiences with established gospel principles and with other people. He began to share the gospel with a friend or two at work and accepted a teaching assignment in his student ward. He found that his attempts to help others understand the gospel increased his own understanding. His renewed appreciation for the many "knowns" in his testimony soon outweighed the "unknowns," and the joy he had earlier felt as a missionary began coming back to him.

Fortunately, he refused to give up when he met opposition. He learned through his struggles and grew stronger. In time a few pieces of the historical puzzle fell into place, but the real turning point came when he stopped being so concerned about his own troubles and began trying to help other people with their troubles. Then he was experiencing the fruits of living the gospel.

Consider what life would be like if we could avoid the opposition we find all around us. If Adam and Eve had remained in the Garden of Eden, protected from the opposition and problems of the lone and dreary world, they would have remained forever "innocent." What does the word *innocent* suggest about the meaning of a Garden-of-Eden kind of life? A good friend once said to me as we parted company, "In case I don't see you again, have a . . . nice life." That is just what we sometimes yearn for—one nice day after another, all adding up to the glorious conclusion of a "nice life." When we are asked at the judgment bar how our life on earth was and what it all means, the following would not be a particularly satisfying answer: "Oh, it was nice. No big problems, really. It was a very nice life."

We once had two beautiful long-haired kittens at our house. Because of the way we pampered and spoiled them, they were living in the Garden of Eden. And they loved it—all that food and warmth and brushing and tender loving care. They didn't even mind being dressed up in Cabbage Patch doll clothes, which was about the worst "opposition" they had to endure. One Saturday morning our kittens (and some of our children) were relaxing sleepily in front of the television set, watching cartoons and purring lightly, enjoying their nice life. As her mother began ordering the television turned off and giving

out assignments to the children for Saturday morning house-
work, our seven-year-old daughter said, "I don't want to do
my work. I would rather be a kitten."

Adam and Eve left the Garden of Eden so that "they might
have *joy*." Not nice days. Not yawning and stretching and loung-
ing in front of a cozy television set throughout eternity. After
Adam and Eve had been in the lone and dreary world long
enough to get some idea of what it meant to "eat bread by the
sweat of thy face" and to "bring forth children in sorrow," an
angel taught them the plan of salvation. By then they had
enough understanding to appreciate what they were taught.
Adam said, "Because of my transgression my eyes are opened,
and in this life I shall have joy." (Moses 5:10.)

Opposition is a central part of mortal life. It is a primary
difference between what life would have been in the Garden
of Eden and what it is in mortality. It is the difference between
being green, untested, and inexperienced versus being ripe,
seasoned, tested, and having a mature perspective. As one of
Shakespeare's characters in *King Lear* says to his father after
they have undergone prolonged, terrible opposition, "Ripeness
is all." Ripeness. Fullness. Richness. How different from innocence; for if there is only innocence, there is but little meaning.

The most important things we can learn in this mortal
probation are learned the slow way, through practice, through
trial and error. This kind of learning actually depends on opposition. Robert Browning understood something about such
a learning process: "There is an answer to the passionate longing of the heart for fullness . . . : live in all things outside yourself
by love and you will have joy. That is the life of God; it ought
to be our life. In Him it is accomplished and perfect; but in
all created things, it is a lesson *learned slowly against difficulty*."[4]

In going off to a Church college, joining the Church, mar-
rying, having children, or serving a mission, we must often
overcome tremendous odds even to embark upon the expe-

rience. For that reason, it is only natural to believe that once we have won the right to the experience, we should live happily ever after. Experiences such as these may surely lead toward living joyfully, but joy—like grace—comes "after all we can do." Indeed, joy—like grace—may well come in the midst of contrary experience, for it is a real part of life. Joy is not an alternative to opposition; it is part of a compound that includes opposition.

We find in the life of President Spencer W. Kimball one further, poignant illustration of that specialized kind of opposition that haunts us even when by all believable odds we should be far beyond it. President Kimball endured a lifelong struggle against physical opposition of many kinds. He experienced so many serious medical problems that he liked to quote a poem about his "friend, pain," because pain had taught him so much.

> *Pain stayed so long I said to him today,*
> *"I will not have you with me any more."*
> *I stamped my foot and said, "Be on your way,"*
> *And paused there, startled at the look he wore.*
> *"I, who have been your friend," he said to me,*
> *"I, who have been your teacher—all you know*
> *Of understanding love, of sympathy,*
> *And patience, I have taught you. Shall I go?"*
> *He spoke the truth, this strange unwelcome guest;*
> *I watched him leave, and knew that he was wise.*
> *He left a heart grown tender in my breast,*
> *He left a far, clear vision in my eyes.*
> *I dried my tears, and lifted up a song—*
> *Even for one who'd tortured me so long.*[5]

President Kimball knew firsthand about joy in the midst of opposition.

Elder Russell M. Nelson had an experience with President Kimball that gives insight into President Kimball's attitude. Elder Nelson, then a renowned heart surgeon, was asked to examine President Kimball in 1972. Then President of the

Council of the Twelve, President Kimball desperately needed open-heart surgery; but Dr. Nelson told the First Presidency that because of his advanced age, there was no medical assurance that the surgery would be successful. When the First Presidency told Elder Kimball they felt he should have the operation despite the risks, Elder Kimball told them his greatest fear was that he might emerge from the surgery in some partially incapacitated state — alive, but unable to do his work. President Kimball's entire life had been a study in conscientious devotion. Carrying more than his share of the load had always been of utmost importance to him.

Following the counsel of President Harold B. Lee, President Kimball submitted to the risky surgery. The Brethren gave Dr. Nelson a special blessing. During the surgery, which proceeded flawlessly, Dr. Nelson received a strong spiritual impression that Elder Kimball would one day be President of the Church. For more than a dozen years after that miraculously successful operation, President Kimball continued on, against all odds, raising his cancer-stricken voice like a beacon in the night.

But he did not live happily ever after. For the last few years of life, he was medically unable to speak to the membership of the Church or to go consistently about his other duties. That which he had feared most came to pass: opposition prevented him from carrying his full share of the load. How his heart must have ached! He must have wondered why the Lord spared his life so many times but then gave him such great responsibility without maintaining his ability to do what his duty seemed to require. If someone as faithful and as "ripe" as President Kimball continued to experience opposition, it is not surprising that the rest of us must as well.

I sensed a very personal kind of love in the tender feelings of Church members for President Kimball during the years of his affliction. There was an appreciative longing for the days when the piercing quality of that unique voice sounded such a clear call at general conference; a kind of loving admiration for his courage — almost of the intimate kind felt only among members of the same family. There was more than a trace of joy and meaning in all this—the kind of meaning that comes from having been together in combat, the kind of joy borne of gratitude for a friend who touched and changed one's life. Taken in such a personal and compassionate context, richer meaning was given to his counsel over earlier years about missions, cleanliness, repentance, and the miracles of both forgiveness and access to the priesthood. The members of the Church were happy and sad at the same time; full of hope yet full of sorrow. It was a mixture of opposing feelings, as God consecrated our afflictions for our gain.

The nature of true joy as part of the rich but rugged texture of reality is reflected in the music of a great composer such as Johannes Brahms, whose exquisite melody lines are hard to pin down or capture. This kind of music—as distinguished from pop tunes—is a more complete and candid reflection of life, mirroring its rich depth and complexity. With the uncertainty and opposition we find in our earthly experience, our moments of joy and happiness—like Brahms' melodies—may rise only briefly beyond the surface and soar fleetingly toward the sun, always against the background of inescapable reality, and then they plunge back into the seas of life—not to be buried, but to be mixed with and enriched by all else that we experience.

In the sad closing scene of the musical *Camelot*, King Arthur finally understands that all is not lost. The emergence of a young boy who believes in the ideals of Camelot shows the power of education: The idea of Camelot will live on even though the physical kingdom is at war. Speaking of this discovery, Arthur says to his friend Pellinore that our lives are like the water that forms the great waves of the sea, moving and swelling for the most part in darkness, but occasionally a few drops break through the air, and as they are caught in the sunlight, some of them sparkle: "Some of them do sparkle, Pelly." And so he sings: "For one brief shining moment, there was a spot—of enlightenment, peace, and security—and that was Camelot." That it happened once offers assurance that it can happen again — perhaps, someday, permanently.

This elusive quality of true joy suggests rather well the conditions of mortality as we know them. The moments of supreme happiness in our lives are not really represented by the carefree, romping frolics of our childhood. Joy is not superficial or cute. It is, rather, represented by moments of understanding and recognition and appreciation that derive their meaning from the backdrop of daily reality, with all its drudgery, its responsibilities, its frustrations, and its tensions. Joy mixed with opposition is like gold mixed with ore. Somehow, our joyful experiences mean more when we are fully conscious of the alternatives and the contrasts that surround us. We prize the sweet more when we have tasted the bitter. We appreciate our health when we see sickness. We truly love peace when we know the ugliness of war. These contrasts do not deter our idealism. Properly understood, they only make the moments of true joy worth waiting for. In this way, punishment and happiness are in opposition — *both* "affixed to answer the ends of the atonement." (2 Nephi 2:10.) And the ultimate end of the Atonement, surrounded by such opposition, is "the great plan of happiness." (Alma 42:8.)

CHAPTER FOUR

A Willingness to Learn from Pain

This chapter continues our exploration of the connections between joy and pain in the mortal experience. We can learn something worthwhile from our experience with spiritual and psychological pain — those pangs of the heart that may come from a wounded conscience, loneliness, disappointment, or a love that is lost.

Anne Morrow Lindbergh is a noted author and the wife of the famous pilot, Charles Lindbergh. The kidnapping of the Lindbergh baby, which finally resulted in the child's death, once captured the attention and sympathy of the American nation. In looking back on her life, Mrs. Lindbergh wrote: "I do not believe that sheer suffering teaches. If suffering alone taught, all the world would be wise, since everyone suffers. To suffering must be added mourning, understanding, patience, love, openness, and *the willingness to remain vulnerable.*"[1] We will all suffer in one way or another, but we need a certain perspective if our suffering is to teach us.

A few years ago our family inherited a dog, a friendly little pup who was all black except for two white paws and a splash of white across his chest. For our three sons he became a real pal. One afternoon I was interrupted at work by a call from home that told a sad story: "Dad! Dad! Our dog is dead!"

"Oh, no!" I said. "I'll be home as soon as I can."

I have seldom seen such looks of gloom as those that met me when I arrived. A motorcycle had come out of nowhere; nobody really knew how it had happened. We laid the rumpled little body to rest in a corner of our backyard in a ceremony that was brief but mournful. I don't know when I've heard so many questions asked all at once about the meaning of the Resurrection. But the answers didn't help; the boys were despondent beyond comfort. As we trudged back to the house, I remembered, but chose not to repeat, what a friend of mine had heard one of his children say on just such an occasion: "Not much of a funeral for such a good dog."

After that experience, my wife and I resisted for a while our children's repeated requests to get another dog. Among the reasons why we were reluctant was our desire to spare our children the grief of another event like losing the black puppy. But we also found ourselves wondering whether the joy of companionship with a puppy would not more than offset that risk.

Many of our decisions are influenced more than they should be by our desire to avoid sorrow, distress, frustration, and other kinds of psychic discomfort. Sometimes we prefer almost anything to that kind of pain.

Our culture has become as skillful in the art of neutralizing emotional and spiritual pain as in sedating physical pain. Medicine is, in a sense, symbolic of our age. Unquestionably, medicine is often a blessing; but the drugs of our time, both the literal and the figurative kinds, also offer escape — not only from pain but also from responsibility and reality. And thus some people have developed an instinctive inclination to chart their course by choosing alternatives that will minimize their exposure to the uncomfortable consequences of taking life as it comes. Avoiding or escaping discomfort becomes a guiding purpose of life, as if getting around such pitfalls were the essence of a happy life.

The gospel teaches, however, that the presence of painful experiences is an important element in man's capacity ultimately to experience joy—and not just because it feels so good when the pain stops. I do not encourage the outright seeking of pain; for it, like temptation, will find us soon enough. Nor can I feel good about the martyr who strangely seems to enjoy and prolong the misery of his misfortunes—the type who is willing to suffer in silence as long as he is sure everybody knows about it. My concern is with those whose priorities and responses seem carefully designed to avoid or escape from psychic pain, almost at any cost.

Consider the pain that comes when our conscience cries out against something we have done or are about to do. There are various ways of responding to that pain. One response tries to outwit the pain by changing one's basic attitudes, even, if necessary, to the point of rejecting God's existence and the validity of moral laws. That change may take some time and effort, but those who have rearranged their view of the universe in just that way have found that somehow the new view makes them more comfortable—because it makes the pain subside. How sad! This change represents only a temporary period of self-deception. Sooner or later we will again see reality as it is and feel the pain all over again, even to "weeping and wailing." In like manner, we may find temporary relief from pangs of conscience by inventing some rational explanation as to why this time what we did was not wrong.

Tragically, those who continually manipulate their conception of reality will discover that while they no longer feel pain when violating some true principle, they also no longer feel the kinds of joy they once knew. What they do not realize is that both their pain and their joy are natural responses to things as they are. Since their highest realizations of joy flow from their accurate perceptions of God's reality and what Enos called "the joy of the saints" (see Enos 1:3), the gradual removal from their mental framework of both God and the saints can gradually remove the joy associated with both.

Of course, those who take this step can still substitute lesser forms of pleasure for what is missing in their lives, so that one who turns his face from God to avoid facing him may still have his fun. But being deprived of true joy is a terrible price to pay to turn off the pain of deserved guilt. Building an entirely new worldview in one's mind in order to *keep* the pain turned off is a formidable task because the universe as it exists is impossible to change.

Fortunately, there is a better alternative. The pain of a wounded conscience comes to us not just to cause suffering. It is an invitation for us to respond in a way that will ultimately lead to joy. To accept the invitation early, we simply need to stop — in midair if necessary — and turn away from whatever we were going to do. If it is too late for that, the invitation of an aroused conscience can still be accepted by a visit with the bishop and by a few other well-known steps of repentance. This approach will eventually stop the pain, but it does so in ways that leave us true to ourselves and to the universe of God's reality. At the same time, our capacity for joy will be undiminished — it may even be enhanced through newly discovered self-control. Then the next time the pain of conscience comes, it will come as the voice of a friend, to tell us those sensitive, sometimes painful kinds of things we would hope a true friend would share. Only when we work through our spiritual pains in this way, rather than avoiding them, will the pain really subside in a way that preserves our sensitivity to joy.

We also encounter forms of psychic pain in the field of formal learning. There are classes or subjects that sometimes seem painfully dull to us. In such circumstances, those who do not sense their own responsibility to read and think and understand may simply turn off. They have grown accustomed to just changing the channel if a learning experience doesn't hold the promise of being fun. It would be far better for them if they could accept the growing pains of discipline, initiative, and determination to stay with a difficult task until it is mastered, until they taste the joy of true understanding. But all of this may sound boring—that ultimate ugliness—to those who believe they have a right to be entertained.

Another kind of emotional pain to which we all seem subject arises from the risks we take in allowing ourselves to love others. There is no suffering quite like that which comes when love is shattered. After years of patient waiting for what seems like the right time, one may open up his or her heart to another, only to find that tender heart bruised or broken when the love is not returned. We therefore bear grave responsibility for the purity of our motives when some trusting heart has offered us entrance. Anyone who stands on that threshold stands on holy ground, ground which must not be exploited or defiled. But should a relationship so develop that, in spite of honesty, caution, and goodness of motive, a parting of the ways still must come, we must not let the pain of that moment make us so resentful or bitter that we become unwilling to risk opening our hearts again. That kind of risk is necessary, because loving simply has its risks. In a sense there is no love without fear.

One of love's fears stems from the continuing possibility that one we love, whether sweetheart, father, child, or sister, may not return after saying good-bye to us one day. Such fear is the constant companion of the wives of combat soldiers— or even the parents of teenagers old enough to drive. I will confess that such fear—such pain—comes over me at times, because of my feelings for those special ones who are in my home. I know that leaves me vulnerable, but it is a risk I am willing to take; its potential for pain is far offset by the abundant joy of love.

There are similar risks in deciding to marry and to bear children. We never know what burdens we may be called upon to bear as a result of those irrevocable commitments. I have seen those who bear such burdens—the husband of the wife who becomes chronically ill, the parents of a malformed child, a person who is called on to care for helpless in-laws. These are the risks of love. But love is worth such risks; these are experiences that can sanctify our love.

There are many other kinds of pain associated with learning what God would have us learn here. There are the growing pains that come from learning through our mistakes. Learning from our own errors requires that we honestly acknowledge them, something that is always painful for those who strive for competence. It is also painful to become as independent as we must be and to learn not to expect others to solve our every problem and meet our every need. It sometimes hurts to be realistic or to wait when patience is required.

The Savior of the world knew all these kinds of pain and many others we canont comprehend. "Man of sorrows" was his name. (See Isaiah 53:3.) Surely he was "acquainted with grief." Only he was capable of absorbing the mental and spiritual anguish inflicted by Gethsemane. As he himself tells us of that pain: how sore we know not, how exquisite we know not, how hard to bear we know not. (See D&C 19:15-19.) Yet when he elsewhere says, "my joy is full" (3 Nephi 17:20), we are assured that a fulness of joy for one such as he must be richer, fuller, and more exquisite than we may ever know in mortality. There is a natural relationship between our capacity to be taught by pain on the one hand and our capacity to receive joy on the other. That is worth remembering when our own pain seems sore and exquisite. (See Alma 36:21.)

There is one other kind of pain of the heart that is familiar to most of us. We call it homesickness. If we feel a little homesick when we are away from home, that is probably a good sign—both about our home and our priorities. Of course, a serious, long-lasting case is probably not healthy for young adults who are gradually being weaned and prepared to build homes of their own. But I mention the idea of homesickness for a larger purpose.

I was once a stake visitor in a sacrament meeting where a member of a temple presidency was talking thoughtfully about the temple. Just before his talk the choir had sung "O My

Father." As he was about to finish, I received a message inviting me to say a few words before the meeting closed. I began reflecting about the temple, asking myself what it really meant to me. I found myself thinking of it in these terms: the temple — a symbol that we are not of this world; a place where earth and heaven meet; a place where homesick children think of home.

The singing of "O My Father" had also stimulated my memory to recall, for some reason, an evening in the home of a warm, bright, and sensitive woman in Germany. As missionaries, we had gone to her home for a peaceful few minutes of refreshment and conversation with her family following their baptism. Because she spoke fluent English, she had added some Tabernacle Choir records to her collection during her investigation of the Church. The records were playing in the background as we sat together and talked about our blessings. When the choir began to sing a beautiful, moving arrangement of "O My Father," we stopped visiting and sat back to listen to the hymn. When it was over, we were all a little misty-eyed.

Then she told us in quiet, reverent tones that listening to this song had been a major turning point in her prayerful quest to receive the restored gospel. She told us about the German word *Sehnsucht*, a poignant, meaningful word that has no exact equivalent in English. I suppose the closest translation would be "a longing for home," but the German word has elements of both longing and searching. She told us that during most of her life she had felt a strange longing for home — a *Sehnsucht* — that had often made her melancholy and at times a little lonely; but she had never been able to identify that for which she longed. She had been impressed with the occasional references to such a feeling in the writings of some European authors, who thought the *Sehnsucht* might have something to do with an innate, almost subconscious human yearning to make contact with the essence of nature and meaning in a universal, cosmic sense.

The first time she heard the choir sing this song, she instinctively knew what her longing was and where it came from: "Yet ofttimes a secret something whispered, 'You're a stranger here,' And I felt that I had wandered from a more exalted sphere. . . . But, until the key of knowledge was restored, I knew not why." Then, "When I leave this frail existence, . . . Father, Mother, may I meet you. . . . "[2] As she described it, I too felt the *Sehnsucht* and knew where it came from.

After relating this story, I shared an agonizing experience I had had that same afternoon interviewing a young couple who wanted to be married in the temple but who were no longer worthy to enter that holy place. As I tried to describe how those two people felt about wanting, in a sense, to go "home" but not being able to go there until completing an arduous repentance process, I found myself thinking about my own longing for home. The almost overpowering thoughts came to me: What if I were unworthy? What if I could never return? What if, after having to turn away my head in shame from that eternal home, I were once again to hear the words, "Father, Mother, may I meet you . . . ? " I really don't think I could stand it. I would spend eternity trying to find some way of shutting off the pain of a longing that could not be fulfilled. Thank heaven — literally — for the Atonement, which promises that, at least on this side of the veil, such exquisite pain need not be permanent.

I will long remember both the words and the feeling expressed by the young man who said the closing prayer in that sacrament meeting: "Please help us, Father. We want to come home."

My present sense of the *Sehnsucht*, as poignant and piercing as it can be, has become the source of my deepest possible motivation. It reminds me that everything but the gospel is temporary. That kind of pain, that kind of homesickness, is a feeling I never want to lose. If I lose it through my rationalizing, through my behavior, or through my treating lightly the things of God, I know that when the great and dreadful day comes when all our knees will bow together, that very pain will return with full-blown and everlasting intensity.

So I want to remain vulnerable to those painful realities that inevitably come with facing the truth, with learning, with growing, and with loving. Pain of that kind helps me remember that I am in contact with life as it was meant to be experienced, thus preparing me more fully for that appointed reunion with those who sent me here—when, at last, my joy may be full.

CHAPTER FIVE

Two Cheers for Excellence

I am not very enthusiastic about lectures and books on "success" and "excellence" among the Latter-day Saints. Much of that material misunderstands, and therefore does not value, the place of apparently "unsuccessful" experience in helping us taste the fruits of both the tree of knowledge and the tree of life. When the bitterness of Adam and Eve's life cycle and the sweetness of the Atonement are working together for our good far beneath the surface, our most sanctifying life experiences will not always look like "success."

I strongly agree with Elder Richard L. Evans, who once told a small Church audience in which I sat, "It is good to be faithful. But how much better it is to be faithful and competent." I share this conviction to the extent of doubting that one is truly faithful if he is less competent than he could be. I know how the leaders of the Church feel about the quality of what is done in the Church Educational System. For instance, I felt the intense concern of President Marion G. Romney about professional quality when the Church created the J. Reuben Clark Law School at BYU. For President Romney, questions by law students about a choice between spiritual excellence and intellectual excellence made no sense at all. Of course, spiritual excellence came first; but to him, as to his great mentor, J.

Reuben Clark, intellectual excellence was simply part of abundant spiritual excellence, and religious devotion was not an acceptable excuse for professional mediocrity.

Yet I feel an ever-deepening uneasiness about our uncritically accepting the assumptions of the Yankee ethic of success, which can be so competitive, self-centered, and superficial. That is why I have only two cheers for excellence. I have reservations not because I believe it justifiable for us to exert less than our finest efforts; rather, I fear that without a wise perspective, an unqualified commitment to "goals" and "excellence" can distort our understanding of certain long-term principles about life and its larger purposes — even if we do put forth great effort.

Consider some examples: I recently talked with a young woman who had unselfishly worked hard at being a good wife and mother through several difficult years of marriage. But now the marriage was breaking down. Her husband had developed emotional problems that seriously threatened the spiritual (and at times even the physical) survival of the woman and her children. Surrounded by many questions, she asked the one that haunted her most: "How could this have happened, when I have tried so hard to do everything the Church has taught me to do?"

Then I talked to a man who had recently joined the Church and found shortly after his conversion that he had a terminal illness. He too had done everything within his power to live as he should, making many sacrifices because of his whole-hearted acceptance of the gospel. With his newly found hopes for life now cut so bluntly short, he could not make sense of it. He wondered aloud, "What have I done wrong?"

One day a young father who had a learning disability and little education asked me a question that he said had worried him for years: "Do you have to be smart and have a good education to get into the celestial kingdom?" I knew him to be a genuine, decent, and hardworking person. He had never tasted of success the way most people measure it and probably never would. As he waited for my answer, I noticed the tears beginning to fill his eyes.

To these people, the high-sounding goal of excellence is not so much a source of motivation as it is a source of frustration and discouragement. They have worked as hard as their circumstances allowed, but the rewards they thought were supposed to accompany great effort somehow eluded them. Not only were they confused about not being rewarded; their failure to achieve had produced feelings of total personal failure.

At a more general level, from the time we are school children, we grow up with grading curves of one kind or another. Because curves by definition have very few real "winners," most people develop a sense of basic inferiority. Most of us aren't among the top 10 percent of anything. Our disappointments range from being the last chosen in a sandlot game to seeing our income range officially designated as "lower middle class" to seeing somebody else always chosen as Mother of the Year.

Yet something fascinates the American public with being Number One. Hugh Nibley has noted that many of us would rather be Number One in hell than a doorkeeper in the House of the Lord. Or, as Satan put it in Milton's *Paradise Lost*, "To reign is worth ambition. Better to reign in Hell than to serve in Heaven."

The competitive environment is all around us. For instance, our younger children were once perpetually confused over the state and national "top ten" rankings among teams in high schools, colleges, and the pros. But they picked up the central message: If you're not "ranked," you must not count for much. So when our sixth grader's basketball team completed its city league schedule without winning a game, all our well meaning advice about the value of learning to play the game fell on deaf and droopy ears. I was reminded of the poem a depressed junior high student wrote after his team got trounced in the district tournament, and certain players' parents made it clear what incompetent wretches the team members were. Said his last line, in a mildly cynical turn of Grantland Rice's old phrase, "They cared not how we played the game, but if we won or lost."

So I cannot help wondering what we are doing to each other in the Church these days, as we subtly but continually reinforce in one another the assumption that tangible and visible "rewards" and "success" are promised those who do what is right or even those who work their hardest. Where does that assumption come from? It certainly is not taught by the gospel. On the contrary, the gospel of Jesus Christ teaches that the lone and dreary world of mortality is soaked through with adversity and trouble—not to torture us, but to teach us.

The gospel promises rewards, but "not as the world giveth, give I unto you." (John 14:27.) Rather, "He who doeth the works of righteousness shall receive his reward, even peace in this world, and eternal life in the world to come." (D&C 59:23.) By contrast, those whose vision is limited to this world measure their success only by being "seen of men." Of such the Savior said, "They have their reward." (Matthew 6:5.)

Despite these plain teachings, the assumptions of contemporary America's success ethic are deeply and powerfully ingrained among many members of the Church. This may be partly the influence of history, as our acceptance of these attitudes has relatively recent origins.

During the first sixty or seventy years after the organization of the Church, there were profound distinctions between the culture of the Latter-day Saints and the culture of America. The Saints had their own ideas, not only about theology but about the total cultural environment, including economic, social, and political systems. During the nineteenth-century heyday of Yankee individualism, "survival of the fittest" was in all its brutality a cherished way of American life. But in the mountain lands of the west, the Great Basin Kingdom of that era was as isolated culturally as it was geographically. Indeed, the Church and its people had been rejected by the melting pot called America in large measure because they would not melt into the pattern of Yankee values. Economically, the Saints sought a deliberate isolation, stressing cooperation among themselves while rejecting the nation's every-man-for-himself brand of free enterprise. Politically, both the City of Joseph Smith (Nauvoo) and the Great Basin of Brigham Young sought a harmony between religious and political life that was never understood by outsiders. Socially, the practice of polygamy became the last straw to a noncomprehending American nation, although it only symbolized a far more fundamental misunderstanding.

After being pushed to the brink of destruction in a story too long to recount here, the Saints ultimately embraced their fellow Americans and worked very hard after the turn of the century to dispel former impressions of their excessive peculiarity. During the twentieth century, the Church and its members became increasingly accepted as a legitimate part of "Main Street, U.S.A." American members of the Church today are often considered among the most ardent defenders of success-oriented, entrepreneurial values.

In some sense, the apparent assimilation of many Church members into the materialistic society of twentieth-century America parallels the assimilation of ancient Israel following its captivity into Babylonian culture. At first the Jewish captives longed to return home to the land and ways of their fathers. But after a time, they had become sufficiently integrated into the larger culture that when the opportunity finally came to return home, most preferred to stay. As observed by the Jewish historian, Ernest Renan:

> Many of the Israelites . . . found themselves very comfortable in Babylonia. Thanks to their practical dexterity, they were able to find a thousand ways of amassing a fortune in a city devoted to luxury and pleasure. . . . They were not at all tempted to . . . return to a narrow strip of land condemned . . . to remain eternally poor.[1]

Similar feelings might be experienced by some Church

members today, who may already be so attached to the ways of modern Babylon that they would be unwilling to leave it.

The competitive ethic of personal success and achievement is one of the chief characteristics of U.S. culture. It is not, therefore, surprising that this set of values would creep into the contemporary attitudes of Latter-day Saints through their embracing of Yankee traditions in the twentieth century. For that reason, a brief glance at the origins of the success ethic in building the American character will help us understand what the ethic is, where it came from, and perhaps what is wrong with it.

The American tradition of worshiping at the altar of excellence is as current as the latest national football poll or hit recording, and as old as the ancient Greeks, whose values America inherited through the European Renaissance: "The central ethical idea in Homer can be found in the instructions that the father of Achilles gives to his son when he sends him off to fight at Troy: 'Always be the best and distinguished above others.' "[2]

The more recent source of this competitive heritage is the Puritan ethic, thought by many historians to have fueled much of the achievement and the rugged individualism of American history. According to the Calvinist theology on which Puritan thought was based, "the elect" of God were chosen totally by predestined divine grace, while all other people remained totally depraved. Because of the antiauthoritarianism that ran through Calvin's teachings, it was not the place of the clergy, civil authorities, or any other human being to judge who had been selected by God's will for salvation. Thus one could feel within his own heart that he had been "chosen" if he saw the fruits of God's grace in his personal affairs—that is, if he were "successful." Such outward evidence also had a way of convincing others of one's divine election. In this way, ideas of religious predestination that seemed to deny free will had the paradoxical effect of creating "a more powerful stimulus to extreme effort and a more moral force than any doctrine of human freedom."³ Thus, "instead of turning to fatalism and resignation," the Puritan ethic "became a challenge to unrelenting effort, a sense of burning conviction, a conviction of having a mission, of . . . being on the side of that Almighty Power which must in the end be everlastingly triumphant."⁴

One other component that emerged in the nineteenth-century doctrine of Yankee self-interest was social Darwinism — the idea that under nature's laws for developing superior characteristics in a species, the triumphs of the strong are "supposed" to emerge amid the disasters of the weak. As described by John D. Rockefeller, one of the presumably successful products of this process, "The American Beauty rose, with all its splendor and fragrance, could not have been produced without sacrificing the buds that grew up around it." In a similar way, the development of a large business that displaces its competition is "merely survival of the fittest . . . the working-out of a law of nature and a law of God."⁵

But there is something wrong with these ideas. A belief in "survival of the fittest" seems to justify the essentially un-Christian idea of putting others down to pull ourselves up. In contrast, the Lord has said: "He that exalteth himself shall be abased, and he that abaseth himself shall be exalted." (D&C 101:42.)

The Calvinist doctrines that underlie the Puritan ethic are even more misleading. Not only does Calvinism deny free agency, it also teaches that our successes are evidence that God has chosen us, while our failures are evidence that God has rejected us. This logic seems compelling enough that those who believe it are more likely to seek success than they are to seek God. At the other extreme, those who experience personal failures can all too easily assume they are the rejects of heaven. When self-doubt of that kind sets in, the will to keep striving may wane. It is natural to assume that when we don't appear to be doing "excellently" the perfection process is not working. But the exact opposite may be true. Our moments of greatest stress and difficulty are often the times when the refiner's fire is doing its most purifying work.

In the stirring story of Job in the Old Testament, Satan, Job's friends, and Job's wife all seemed to believe in some variation on the theme of the Puritan ethic. Satan claimed at the beginning of the story that the only reason for Job's obedience was that God had blessed him with much prosperity. Who wouldn't fear God, he suggested, when doing so obviously advances one's materialistic self-interest? In response, God sent adversity to Job, with a fury that appeared unfair. It certainly seemed unfair to Job's wife, whose assumption that God had rejected them was matched by her assumption that their only alternative was to reject God.

Job's friends took the view that anybody with Job's problems must obviously have brought them upon himself by unrighteousness. "Who ever perished, being innocent?" (Job 4:7.) So they urged him to repent of whatever he was doing to anger God, promising an immediate return to prosperity as the reward: "If thou return to the Almighty, thou shalt. . . . have plenty of silver." (Job 22:23, 25.) But Job had the insight they lacked about the nature of both God's love and the mortal experience: "If I have made gold my hope. . . . this also were an iniquity." (Job 31:24, 28.) Job understood that the only reliable constant in life is our relationship with God, with whatever combination of joy and affliction may be ours in that relationship: "The Lord gave, and the Lord hath taken away; blessed be the name of the Lord." (Job 1:21.) "Till I die I will not remove mine integrity from me. . . . For what is the hope of the hypocrite, though he hath gained, when God taketh away his soul? Will God hear his cry when trouble cometh upon him? Will he delight himself in the Almighty? will he always call upon God? . . . But where shall wisdom be found? and where is the place of understanding? Man knoweth not the price thereof. . . . It cannot be gotten for gold. . . . Behold, the fear of the Lord, that is wisdom; and to depart from evil is understanding. But he knoweth the way that I take: when he hath tried me, I shall come forth as gold." (Job 27:5, 8-10; 28:12-13, 15, 28; 23:10.)

I am addressing primarily a need for perspective. I do not

mean to diminish the value of serious commitments to personal achievement and responsibility. The willingness to strive and keep striving is at the heart of Job's message to us. But the striving must be to find out God and to accept fully the experiences he knows will enlarge our souls. The trouble with modern pursuits of excellence is that they can become a striving to please other people, or at least to impress them or to seek their approval. A desire for such approval is not all bad, especially among Church members, who generally reserve their approval for accomplishments having positive value. But other people are not finally our judge, and making too much of either the affirmative or the adverse judgments of others can actually undermine our relationship with God and our development of sound values.

There are many ways in which our natural desire for the approval and praise of other people can distort our perspective. For example, today's society gives great prominence to financial success and public visibility. However, as stated by Elder Boyd K. Packer, "It is the misapprehension of most people that if you are good, really good at what you do, you will eventually be both widely known and well compensated. . . . The world seems to work on that premise. The premise is false. It is not true. The Lord taught otherwise. You need not be either rich or hold high position to be completely successful and truly happy. . . . We want our children and their children to know that the choice of life is not between fame and obscurity, nor is the choice between wealth and poverty. The choice is between good and evil. That is a very different matter indeed."[6]

Joseph F. Smith, the sixth President of the Church, once expressed the same attitude in these words: "True greatness consists in doing well the things God has ordained as the common lot of mankind."[7]

But, as our society has become more materialistic, our vision has been blurred on many issues of meaning and value. One of the tragedies of today's emphasis on careers, for example, has been the growing public attitude that unless society places some tangible economic value on childrearing and household labor, such labor is of questionable worth. One result of this assumption is that both women and men increasingly believe they should measure life's satisfactions in terms of professional or other "career" accomplishments. This premise has found its way into virtually every corner of public discourse these days.

The effect of emphasizing individual gain on our view of domestic priorities was captured by BYU anthropologist Merlin Myers:

> Members of society are important, not in terms of their kinship relations, but rather in terms of their success in getting gain. . . . For us, gain — most often reckoned in monetary terms — is the measure of social worth and status. The begetting, bearing, and caring for children does not produce gain in the currently accepted sense of the word. Rather, this [childrearing] may put strain on what gain is available, or may impede the freedom and mobility of a person in his or her quest for gain. Women are thus caught in the very unenviable position of having the most decisive attributes of their femininity, or womanhood, denigrated by the society in which they live as being an obstacle to their achieving worth. . . . Day-care centers and old people's homes . . . free those who would be responsible for children and parents in societies where kinship norms prevail, to pursue personal gain in one form or another. . . . (Compare this with the statement of the heart-rent Rachel to her husband, Jacob, "Give me children else I die!")[8]

Another distortion in our thinking about personal achievement is our inability to see that many forms of apparent success and apparent failure result from causes beyond our control. For that reason, it is not always fair to impute responsibility for triumph or disaster to those who seem to have found them.

(Rudyard Kipling's "If" expresses the hope that we may "meet with Triumph and Disaster and treat those two imposters just the same.") During my experience as a practicing lawyer, I encountered many people whose business success was more the result of good guesses, good connections, and favorable market conditions than the result of great attributes of personal character or even good management. On the other hand, I knew a number of fine people who appeared to "fail" temporarily because of business conditions or other forces quite beyond their control.

I have made a similar observation on college campuses. A common problem among students is lack of self-esteem. Many reasons for low morale are readily apparent: not having a nice car, or not having a car at all; not having lots of friends or nice clothes or a big scholarship; not enjoying a position of prominence in campus life; feeling socially unsuccessful or intellectually inferior; feeling too poor or too plain in appearance. Students on large campuses often feel discouraged and overwhelmed by the daily process of being graded (as if in some eternal sense) by relentless examinations, papers, and grading curves. Many of the obstacles to success in the campus environment, as elsewhere, are from sources beyond the control of the student, whether that is one's native intelligence, looks, or family wealth. The most frustrating feelings, not only about one's belief in oneself but also about one's belief in the fairness of life, come from the hopelessness of trying to control forces that are simply beyond our reach.

Reinhold Neibuhr's oft-quoted advice is worth pondering: "God, give us the serenity to accept what cannot be changed, courage to change what should be changed, and the wisdom to distinguish the one from the other."

From God's perspective on our lives, we can control the things that really matter: the righteousness of our desires, the purity of our motives, the wholeheartedness of our efforts to love God and keep his commandments, the genuineness of our interest in other people, and the extent to which our efforts reflect our inborn capacity. One way to distinguish what matters a great deal from what does not matter so much is to ask whether the subject is within our control. If it is, then it probably matters enough to merit our attention. But if the object of our fretting is inherently beyond our control, God is unlikely to hold us responsible for our ultimate success or failure as to that concern.

Our perspective can also be impaired by assuming that achievement in one area of endeavor establishes some general level of merit or worth. However, no specialized success can compensate for weaknesses of character. Moreover, all people represent some combination of strengths and limitations. As Elder Richard L. Evans once said, "Nobody has everything that everyone else has." As a young teenager I didn't understand that. I somehow got the idea that all people were "ranked" along some vertical scale from really being somebody to not counting for much. I gradually came to understand, as I came to know the private lives of more people over time, that each of us has been given some spiritual gift that is uniquely our own. "To every man is given a gift by the spirit of God." (D&C 46:11.) Further, each of us has weaknesses and limitations that are sufficient to keep us modest. As the Lord told Moroni, "I give unto men weakness that they may be humble." (Ether 12:27.) Each person represents some particular combination of gifts and limitations as we stand on a horizontal plane with one another. But the heroes of public attention are shown to us by the media as if they were superhuman in every respect.

Finally, our preoccupation with achievement as society defines it focuses our attention on other people rather than on God, as our judge. However, not only is popular opinion too fickle and fleeting to serve as a reliable guide for our self-worth, but others cannot possibly know enough about our hearts and the innermost elements of our lives to judge us fairly. Also, men's standards of judgment are not sound, because they lack the perspective of eternity. Thus our dependence upon outward signs of success and our vulnerability to adverse judgments by others can divert us from establishing a relationship with the only One whose judgment ultimately matters very much.

The Apostle Paul wrote to the Romans, "And we know that all things work together for good to them that love God." (Romans 8:28.) If we do all within our power to love God, the doctrines of mercy and Atonement allow him to ensure that all the circumstances of our lives will eventually "work together" for our best good.

This proposition is different from the Pollyanna-like assumption that because we are children of God all things will work out for the best. More is required of us than that. For us the requirement is to love God—to love him with all our heart, might, mind, and strength. That is no trivial task. For, "He that hath my commandments, and keepeth them, he it is that loveth me." (John 14:21.) It is a devotion that asks for all our hearts. "Jesus answered him, Wilt thou lay down thy life for my sake?" (John 13:38.) Joseph Smith described this same attitude in terms of the principle of sacrifice: One who offers "in sacrifice all that he has for the truth's sake, not even withholding his life," is in a position to know when his life choices are pleasing to God.[9]

Significantly, this single-minded devotion is within our control. It does not depend upon our talents, our heritage, our looks, or our intelligence. And the completeness of our love cannot be judged by others—they are likely to know very little about it. For this is a love too private, too intimate and sacred to be seen of men, much less judged by them. There is only one judge, and on the fairness of his judgment we can surely rely. For "the keeper of the gate is the Holy One of Israel; and he employeth no servant there." (2 Nephi 9:41.)

If we love God in this sense, even though we are not perfect and even though we may not be thought of as successful or excellent by others, the promise is that—while not without our effort, not always quickly, and not always as we might predict—all things will work together for our good.

Through the miracle of the Atonement and through the grace and power of the Savior, this means that—if our repentance is complete—he will compensate for our failures, our sins, and our mistakes. It further means that he will perfect us—make us truly excellent—beyond our power to perfect ourselves.

All things working together for our good is very different from all things working together for our apparent success or excellence as measured by the standards of this world. Because his making us perfect enough to enjoy eternal life is our ultimate goal, we may need all things to work "for our good" in such a way that there are growing pains, tests, afflictions, and the purification by fire. "As many as I love, I rebuke and chasten." (Revelation 3:19.) This need for discipline may bring us experiences others would not judge to be big success stories. We may have encounters that are harsh, painful, and beyond our ability (let alone the ability of other people) to understand.

To develop a sufficiently independent relationship with God requires that the private world in which we dwell in communion with him transcend the other "worlds" we inhabit—the world of work, community life, friends, family, and even relationships in the Church. As we gain experience in that private and personal world, we will become less dependent upon the approval of others for our sense of personal worth. As that happens, we will come to understand what Hugh Nibley meant when he said:

> I have always been furiously active in the Church, but I have . . . never held an office or rank in anything; I have undertaken many assignments given me by the leaders of the Church, and much of the work has been anonymous. No rank, no recognition, no anything. While I have been commended for some things, they were never the things which I considered most important—that was entirely a little understanding between me and my Heavenly Father, which I have thoroughly enjoyed, though no one else knows anything about it.[10]

An image suggesting this kind of private relationship with the Lord is described in a story by Robert Louis Stevenson. Stevenson tells of his boyhood, growing up in a part of England where darkness came early in the evening. He and his friends imitated British policemen by carrying small, tin "bull's-eye" lanterns on their belts. Just for the fun of it, Stevenson and his friends made a game out of hiding the glowing lantern inside the front of their buttoned overcoats and then making their way along the dark paths as if they had no light with them. In Stevenson's words:

> When two of these [lads] met, there would be an anxious, 'Have you got your lantern?' and a gratified 'Yes!' That was the shibboleth, and very needful, too; for, as it was the rule to keep our glory contained, none could recognize a lantern-bearer unless (like the polecat) by the smell. . . . The essence of this bliss was to walk by yourself in the black night, the slide shut, the top-coat buttoned, not a ray escaping, whether to conduct your footsteps or to make your glory public, — a mere pillar of darkness in the dark; and all the while, deep down in the privacy of your fool's heart, to know you had a bull's-eye at your belt, and to exult and sing over the knowledge. . . .
>
> [One's] life from without may seem but a rude mound of mud: [but] there will be some golden chamber at the heart of it, in which he dwells delighted; and for as dark as his pathway seems to the observer, he will have some kind of bull's-eye at his belt.[11]

Stevenson then describes the ultimate subjectivity of true joy, noting that other people simply cannot fully appreciate the innermost delights and sorrows of our lives. He suggests that if we could only experience forms of joy quickly perceived and acknowledged by others, that kind of joy would fall far short of the high forms of happiness and insight of which the human soul is capable.

Since our highest forms of joy (and, I suppose, our deepest moments of sorrow) are beyond the realm of ordinary speech, one great purpose served by music, art, poetry, and dance is to free us for a broader realm of personal expression. In Stevenson's words, "Only the poets find out where the joy resides, and give it a voice far beyond singing." Yet this private kind of joy, impossible to communicate objectively to others, is so significant in the human experience that "to miss the joy is to miss all. In the joy of the actors lies the sense of any action. That is the explanation, that the excuse. To one who has not the secret of the lanterns, the scene [of the boys in the dark] is meaningless."[12] If we understand the secret of the lanterns, we will not miss the joy that awaits us in discovering that all things do work together for good to them who love God. Others may not always understand what happens in this private world of our relationship with God. This means, of course, that they may be unlikely to applaud us or comfort us in those moments when we are most in need of being understood and appreciated. But if we love God, we have the assurance of knowing that he understands and sustains us, and the uninformed judgments of others, whether negative or positive, cannot come between us and God. "For I am persuaded, that neither death, nor life, nor angels, nor principalities, nor powers, nor things present, nor things to come, nor height, nor depth, nor any other creature, shall be able to separate us from the love of God, which is in Christ Jesus our Lord." (Romans 8:38-39.)

If we were to let our thoughts be drawn out toward the heavens enough to transcend, even temporarily, the strains and limitations of daily life, we would be likely to hear the promptings of him who overcame all things, assuring us that the promise is true: He will, as an act of mercy, cause the circumstances of our lives to be for our ultimate blessing, if only we love him with all our hearts. There is no grading on a curve here: "He that overcometh, the same shall be clothed in white raiment; and I will not blot out his name out of the book of life, but I will confess his name before my Father, and before

his angels. I know thy works: behold, I have set before thee
an open door, and no man can shut it: for thou hast a little
strength, and has kept my word, and hast not denied my name.
Because thou hast kept the word of my patience, I also will
keep thee from the hour of temptation, which shall come upon
all the world. . . . Him that overcometh will I make a pillar in
the temple of my God, and he shall go no more out: and I will
write upon him the name of my God . . . and I will write upon
him my new name." (Revelation 3:5, 8, 10, 12.)

To feel this assurance is to sense the reward of peace in
this world and the promise of eternal life in the world to come.
This is a more excellent way.

CHAPTER SIX

Obedience, Sacrifice, and a Contrite Spirit

During recent years, I have noticed the increasingly frequent occurrence of two problems among LDS college students: first, those who demand too much of themselves; and second, those who do not demand enough of themselves. After thinking these two problems had nothing in common — in fact, they seem to be opposites to each other — I now see a common root. Some of us may even find ourselves in both categories at once.

Let us first consider the perfectionists, those who make extremely high demands of themselves. A recently returned missionary came to see me one day. He felt like a failure and was discouraged to the point of despondency. He had joined the Church just two or three years before going on his mission. His conversion had led to major changes in his life-style, but he had welcomed the new perspective. It had given him a fresh and meaningful sense of purpose about his education, his relationships with young women, and his very reasons for existing. His mission had been the most exhilarating and rewarding experience of his life. He had responded so positively to that highly disciplined environment that the idea of setting and reaching personal goals had become his primary motivating force. He had developed great confidence in his ability to achieve whatever standard or task he set for himself. In addition, he had come to enjoy (even bask in) the adulation of Church members and younger missionaries among whom his influence and leadership had been a positive force. All these sources of psychic reinforcement had made the latter part of his mission a "spiritual high."

At the end of his mission, this young man returned home with a strong sense of buoyancy and optimism about himself and his future prospects. Shortly after his return, he met an attractive young woman at a church function. They began falling in love, and the power of it all drew him into intimacies that seemed irresistible. After the first mistake of a serious kind, he was so shocked at his own behavior that he was plunged into a sea of self-doubt. That experience led to another, and his self-doubt grew to overwhelming self-condemnation. His former sense of confidence and direction was totally shattered, and he became convinced that he lacked the capacity to live as he should. In his own mind he was simply not celestial material. He essentially threw up his hands and said to himself, "What's the use. I've just been kidding myself about all this progress since joining the Church." Once he reached that point, he had lost all motivation to live as he should, and his behavior began to reflect that change. Fortunately, he finally caught himself before this spiritual free-fall had destroyed him—but not before coming perilously close to losing all he had come to live for.

Once a person has seriously committed himself to the high personal standards taught by the gospel, it is easy to believe there are only two categories—blemished and unblemished. The trouble with such categorial thinking, however, is that one or two blemishes can appear to taint us as negatively as a hundred blemishes. Two drops of ink in a pool of pure water can seem to create a polluted pool, just as surely as would a whole bottle full of ink.

A young father was taking his turn with a new baby in the wee hours of the night. The father, already very tired, was under great pressure to complete a demanding school assignment early the next morning, and needed all the sleep he could get. The baby was unusually fussy, however, and none of the father's sleep-inducing tactics worked at all: he walked the baby, burped him, sang to him, rubbed him gently, and fed him warm milk. After an hour, the young man picked up the baby firmly and spoke to him through clenched teeth as if the baby were a fifteen-year-old: "Go to sleep, darn you!" he insisted intensely. The baby only began to howl. As the father returned the baby to his crib, his frustration was suddenly replaced by a wave of shame. He knew the infant had some unknown irritation and was hardly keeping him awake on purpose. He knelt by the crib and prayed for forgiveness. But for some time afterward, he found himself wading through feelings of self-doubt. He had prided himself in believing he was becoming a good father. Now he questioned whether he was the kind of person he wanted to be and often appeared to be. He wondered if his outwardly mature and upstanding appearance were just a facade, masking a character that was more selfish and immature.

Another young man was beginning to experience an increasing commitment to the Church, and he felt a new awareness of the needs of other people. He found himself able to help others who needed him and discovered an inner satisfaction in his emerging ability to control immature tendencies that had plagued him as a teenager. During a week in which everything seemed to be going extremely well, in a thoughtless moment he divulged a personal confidence that led to his severe personal embarrassment. His reaction was that this error "spoiled everything," and he began to doubt whether the other areas of progress in his life were really what they appeared to be.

A sensitive and alert woman found herself in a situation in which other people were acting inappropriately. In an effort to help, she found an indirect way to say something to a Church leader without disclosing enough information to harm any individual. Her comments were misunderstood, and she became tangled in a complex pattern of personal relationships that became impossible to resolve to the satisfaction of all concerned. She felt she had lost the confidence of the Church leader as well as her friends, but reassured herself that her own integrity was intact. Then, when the problem remained unresolved, she began to see herself through the eyes of those who had misjudged her, even though their perceptions were inaccurate. At that point she started losing confidence in herself and in the validity of her judgments.

I know two individuals whose spouses died. There were differing circumstances in each case, but both of the surviving companions were people of extraordinary devotion and loyalty. They attended to the needs of their loved ones with absolute fidelity and unselfishness, showing a constant willingness to sacrifice their own needs, time, and resources when doing so could help their companions in their months and years of final illness. Yet in each case the survivors felt they should have done something that might have given additional comfort or even prolonged life somewhat longer. They judged themselves very harshly for not doing more.

Some of these people are such noble stalwarts that their unhappiness with themselves in these situations calls to mind the example of Nephi. After Lehi's death, Nephi assumed the prophetic leadership role with the extended family. Nephi had already experienced mighty visions and other miraculous manifestations of the Spirit. He had endured many afflictions, being assured in the midst of his trials, as he was in his spiritual experiences, of the Lord's interest in him. Yet, perhaps because of this very progress along the path toward perfection, the seasoned and mature Nephi was acutely conscious of his own limitations: "Notwithstanding the great goodness of the Lord, in showing me his great and marvelous works, my heart exclaimeth: O wretched man that I am! . . . I am encompassed about, because of the temptations and the sins which do so easily beset me. . . . nevertheless, I know in whom I have trusted. . . . Awake, my soul! No longer droop in sin. . . . May the

112

gates of hell be shut continually before me, *because that my heart is broken and my spirit is contrite!*" (2 Nephi 4:17-19, 28, 32; emphasis added.)

The nearer we approach the holiness we seek, the more conscious we become of the blemishes that mark our human-ness. Perhaps that very humiliating consciousness is part of what it means to have a broken heart and a contrite spirit.

Yet when we think, consciously or not, that success and failure are the only alternative outcomes, we will define any outcome short of total success to mean failure. Because almost no human activity or venture is an unqualified success, this means that most of what we do will seem to partake more of failure than success. If we are both honest with ourselves and committed to high principles, there will always be some dis-tance between where we are and where we wish we were. But it can be very difficult to live with an awareness of that distance. This is particularly true when, after some kind of inadequate performance on our part, we solemnly promise ourselves, the Lord, or others that we will never falter again. Such a pledge — even though it may be the right thing to do — can set us up for trouble later on. Long-term personal growth in the natural human environment is usually accomplished by a gradual movement in the right direction, even though there may be ups and downs along the way. In the short run, however, any "downs" seem magnified out of proportion — perhaps partly because we always worry that any small or temporary change in direction may be the beginning of a permanent new trend.

I have a certain skepticism about students who have a 4.0 grade point average in college. I can't help wondering if they have deliberately avoided demanding courses of study. I also have little sympathy for those in this category who receive their first A-. I have seen them in tears at that blessed event. My reaction is to tell them, "Well, your shiny new car has its first dent. Now you can get along with your journey like the rest of us, concentrating on the sights and sounds of your travels without worrying about your car getting dusty along the bumpy road. Welcome to real life."

There was only one who was unblemished and without spot. Perhaps the scriptural phrases that describe the Savior in this way were chosen deliberately, as the total absence of any spot or blemish characterizes no other mortal. If we can think of ourselves along some broad spectrum that ranges from greatly blemished to slightly blemished, we may thus be seeing things more accurately than we do when clean and dirty are the only alternative descriptions.

Consider now those who do not demand enough of themselves. Their problem is very different from that of the perfectionists. This group could be described in a variety of ways. Some of them are simply lazy; others don't seem to know what it means to live according to any standard that makes them stretch or reach very much. I am thinking primarily of those who believe they are entitled to a few "free ones" before any penalties apply.

The phrase "one free bite" comes from the annals of personal injury law and means that the owner of a dog is not held legally responsible when his animal bites a stranger, unless the owner is on notice from past experience that his dog has a propensity to bite. I have heard the term *free ones* used with increasing frequency, however, among college-age men and women in the Church who face judgments of their worthiness. It is common practice for young adults to be interviewed by a bishop or other Church authority in connection with applications to attend a Church college, go on a mission, or be married in the temple. There was a time when it was highly unusual for young people who were really interested in such opportunities to ever be denied them as a result of personal unworthiness. But as the moral standards of the surrounding culture have deteriorated in recent years, more members of the Church have been confronted with serious problems and temptations. The number of people who have been temporarily or permanently denied the higher privileges of Church membership, and the number subjected to Church discipline, have correspondingly increased.

Through this accumulated experience, informal channels of communication have had a way of suggesting how much wrongdoing is likely to be considered "really wrong," in the sense of causing privileges to be withheld. In addition, the concept of repentance unfortunately is often discussed "by the numbers," or in other terms that somehow suggest a kind of mechanistic approach—something like, it's all right to sin as long as you are sure you really repent immediately afterward.

In this environment, one occasionally hears of college-age young people who yield completely to physical temptations, while playing little games with definitions and rules they believe will allow a safe answer to questions about moral worthiness. Others, it is said, will carefully watch the nature and number of their deliberate offenses, so that even when they acknowledge certain difficulties they will not be threatened with serious penalties or disabilities.

This pattern prompts a memory of some youngsters in a small community who ordered a gigantic box of powerful fireworks through the mail. When the box arrived, they devised a strategy to allow them to explode all the devices without violating local laws against such things. The most penitent-looking of their number was elected to take a handful of the tamest firecrackers to the local sheriff and turn himself in. Just as the boys had hoped, the soft-hearted sheriff was so touched that he said, "I'm so proud of you for honestly bringing me those illegal firecrackers that I'm going to let you set them off out by the city dump." The boys gathered up all the fireworks and went to the designated sanctuary to set off the entire illegal assortment in a big party of triumph. Their ingenious plan had worked.

One hears also, now and then, of prospective missionaries who chart the number of weeks before their final interviews or other deadlines, then decide what they can safely do to "live it up" in one last binge of freedom. This frame of mind was reflected in the experience of two brothers, ages seven and nine. The seven-year-old was apprehended by his father while carrying a small amount of money he had taken without permission. The father sat down with his boy for a solemn talk about stealing. After listening patiently for a few minutes, the little boy said innocently, "But, dad, Alan (his nine-year-old brother) says it's okay to steal things until you're eight!" The father then asked Alan, the young theologian, why he would tell his little brother it was all right to steal things until he's eight. Said the nine-year-old with confidence, "That's what I told him, and it's right. When he's eight, he'll be baptized and all his sins will be washed away. So I say—live it up!"

It is one thing to recall the relative innocence of younger children who gradually must learn to confront the reality of rules and commandments. But when adults of any age view transgression in much the same way, they are misunderstanding something fundamental about the nature and purpose of divine expectations. If such doctrinal near-sightedness is not corrected, it will eat away at the foundations of faith and testimony until there is nothing left—regardless of how one might have been spared by a few technicalities in an interview.

There is some risk in even discussing these two problems in the same context. If perfectionists are given advice intended to make them less demanding of themselves, the freeloaders may take that advice as license to redefine even more liberally the boundaries that limit their conduct. Conversely, if the undisciplined ones are scolded for not demanding enough of themselves, those in the first group may be made to feel even worse about their minor blemishes, whatever they are.

Yet both groups share some common misconceptions. For instance, both reflect a low tolerance for pain and discomfort. I have noticed lately how my children seem to require their own built-in, customized thermostats to be sure that their environment never becomes uncomfortable at either extreme. They also dislike boredom, and their standards for deciding whether a proposed event sounds exciting seem to rise ever higher. In such a frame of mind, the first sign of discomfort causes people with rigidly high standards to have very little patience with the source of their irritation—which is often themselves. They feel much too muddy at the first sign of a smudge, having grown accustomed to daily showers.

Similarly, the fun-loving, permissive types feel strongly about romping in the mud right up to the moment they must take their spiritual shower of repentance. For them, enjoying the excitement of a few free ones until the moment of a deadline seems their rightful due. But those who walk too close to the edge of a no-fault, guaranteed romping time may find that they cannot wash every stain from their clothes and hands. They may discover too late, as did Shakespeare's tragic Lady Macbeth, that there is not enough water in the ocean to wash their hands of the consequences of their wrongful deeds. Lady Macbeth went insane with maddened washing, crying: "Here's the smell of the blood still. All the perfumes of Arabia will not sweet this little hand. Oh, oh, oh!"

This is not to say that repentance doesn't work in the spiritual sense. It does and it can, when it is genuine. But the "entanglements" of sin (see D&C 88:86)—the bent fenders and the broken hearts, the addictions and the lost opportunities, the unwanted children and the unfortunate marriages, the bills to pay and the fences to mend—these may never wash away.

There is an even more fundamental problem common to those who are too tough on themselves and those who are not tough enough. Both reflect a basic shallowness in their understanding of the purpose behind the commandments, the significance of one's internal motivation, and the meaning of the Atonement. At issue is their comprehension of the law of obedience and sacrifice—specifically, their readiness to offer the Lord a broken heart and a contrite spirit.

Joseph Smith spoke of the importance of one's knowledge "that the course of life which he pursues is according to the will of God." The prophet taught that such knowledge is nec-

117

essary "to enable him to have that confidence in God without which no person can obtain eternal life." He continued:

> A religion that does not require the sacrifice of all things never has power sufficient to produce the faith necessary unto life and salvation; for, from the first existence of man, the faith necessary unto the enjoyment of life and salvation never could be obtained without the sacrifice of all earthly things.... It is through the medium of the sacrifice of all earthly things that men do actually know that they are doing the things that are well pleasing in the sight of God. When a man has offered in sacrifice all that he has for the truth's sake, not even withholding his life, and believing before God that he has been called to make this sacrifice because he seeks to do his will, he does know, most assuredly, that God does and will accept his sacrifice and offering, and that he has not, nor will not, seek his face in vain....
>
> But those who have not made this sacrifice to God do not know that the course which they pursue is well pleasing in his sight; for whatever may be their belief or their opinion, it is a matter of doubt and uncertainty in their mind.... [And] persons whose minds are under doubts and fears cannot have unshaken confidence; and where unshaken confidence is not there faith is weak; and where faith is weak the persons will not be able to contend against all the opposition ... and afflictions which they will have to encounter in order to be ... joint heirs with Christ Jesus; and they will grow weary in their minds, and the adversary will have power over them and destroy them.[1]

The second paragraph of the above statement describes the underlying problem of *both* those who are too demanding of themselves and those who are not demanding enough: They do *not* know that the course they pursue is pleasing to God, and they lack that confidence in God without which there is insufficient faith to obtain eternal life. Moreover, both lack the attitude of sacrifice of which the prophet spoke. The sacrificial attitude is that we want nothing else more than we want eternal life. It is the attitude of a broken heart and a contrite spirit. Let us apply these observations to both groups.

The returned missionary in the first illustration came home from his mission on a "spiritual high" made up primarily of confidence in himself. That was the confidence shattered by his mistakes after he returned home. Joseph Smith had much to say about confidence in his *Lectures on Faith,* but he spoke of confidence in God, not confidence in oneself—"that confidence in God without which no person can obtain eternal life." That same confidence is mentioned in another revelation given through the Prophet Joseph: "Let virtue garnish thy thoughts unceasingly; then shall thy *confidence* wax strong in the presence of God; and the doctrine of the priesthood shall distill upon thy soul as the dews from heaven. The Holy Ghost shall be thy constant companion. . . . " (D&C 121:45-46; emphasis added.)

Part of the sacrifice of a broken heart and a contrite spirit is a willingness to sacrifice the love affair so many of us have with our own egos. One of the hazards of introducing modern methods of salesmanship into our missionary efforts (methods that do serve some constructive purposes) is that young missionaries may be induced to believe they can do anything they make up their minds to do. Even when they superficially "give the credit to God" for their achievements, too many of them end up believing that they are wonderful missionaries, teachers, leaders, and examples because they have "reached their goals" and are thus models of achievement. To reach a "spiritual high" under these circumstances may be, in some sense, a self-congratulatory feeling of triumph that feels so good because it makes us look so good.

Blemishes and mistakes are natural. They are part of the process of growth through which we all must pass. When we establish criteria for measuring success that somehow system-

119

atically eliminate the complex areas of life in which we may learn most from our errors, we are creating an artificial world that prospers by measuring the measurable and achieving the achievable, rather than by dealing honestly with our most genuine growth experiences.

But when we place our confidence in God rather than in ourselves, our need for self-esteem takes care of itself—not because of our manipulation of successful experiences but because our fundamental attitude allows us access to the only trustworthy source for knowing that the course of life we pursue is known to and accepted by God. It is not just the mistake-free, no-fault life that pleases God. He has deliberately placed us in a sphere where the most sharply focused purpose is to learn from our experience and to grow in both our desires and our understanding to be like him. Obviously that includes the greatest effort and integrity we can muster as we seek to do his will. But the heart of it all is not *self*-confidence. It is confidence in *him*, and in his power to make us into creatures far beyond the reach of what our goal-setting and goal-achieving can ultimately accomplish in the process of becoming as he is.

When our sacrificial attitude includes the willingness to sacrifice our preoccupation with having a contented ego, we are likely at least to be humble about our mistakes. That is a very different matter from never making any mistakes. When our hearts are right and our confidence is in God, the mistakes we make, such as they are, will at least tend to be honest ones. They may also be foolish mistakes at times, but they will not be mistakes borne of calculated attempts to fool God, our leaders, or ourselves. Our mistakes will, then, not destroy us or make us despondent. Indeed, the Lord will make the mistakes of honest, God-fearing people ultimately work for their good. He does this by helping us grow in the midst of our inadequacy and become better able to appreciate the sweet as we overcome the bitter.

Moroni was more than a little bit preoccupied with his

own inadequacies in expressing the written word. He felt he was far more "mighty" in his spoken language. (Reading Moroni's description of his frustration makes us wish we could hear him on an audio tape.) Said the Lord to Moroni, "And if men come unto me I will show unto them their weakness. I give unto men weakness that they may be humble; and my grace is sufficient for all men that humble themselves before me; for if they humble themselves before me, and have faith in me, then will I make weak things become strong unto them." (Ether 12:27.)

Through the power of the Atonement, the Savior himself compensates ultimately for our inadequacies, even as he leads us along and strengthens our capacity for good. For that reason *he* is the desired repository of our confidence. To repose our confidence in ourselves rather than in him is to trust in the arm of flesh, a source of meager and unreliable confidence. Perhaps that is why Nephi concluded his lament, quoted earlier, which finally became a song of praise to God: "O Lord, I have trusted in thee, and I will trust in thee forever. I will not put my trust in the arm of flesh; for . . . cursed is he that putteth his trust in man or maketh flesh his arm." (2 Nephi 4:34.)

Now we must apply the sacrificial attitude to those who want a few free sins. A broken heart and a contrite spirit create a completely different motivation and intent than are present with those who think the commandments are hoops we must jump through or lines arbitrarily drawn to keep our pleasure-seeking at bay. One who has an attitude of honest humility really is willing to give up everything—even his sins. If he cannot bring himself to part with his secret earthly pleasures, he is indeed far from the frame of mind without which he cannot possibly have confidence in God, knowledge of where he stands with him, or the faith necessary to make spiritual progress.

Those who make only modest or casual demands on themselves are always in doubt, not only about their standing before God, but about their understanding of God. They always wonder where the line is beyond which they should not go. They always need someone else to tell them what the "rules" are, because they lack the relationship with God from which a perception about the nature and purpose of commandments can come. Perhaps the need to be forever wondering when one has "gone too far" is related to the problem of seeking for a sign. There have always been those who said they would believe if shown a sign. These the Lord called a wicked and adulterous generation, perhaps because they—like those who wish consciously to err right up to the edge of the line—wish to get away with "whatever is allowed," right up to the point of confronting a tangible sign that draws unavoidable lines.

The essential desire to get away with something is evidence of internal unholiness. For these shallow-minded ones, the Prophet Joseph Smith's description is especially true: "Whatever may be their belief or their opinion, it is a matter of doubt and uncertainty in their mind . . . [and they] cannot have unshaken confidence." Therefore, "they will grow weary in their minds, and the adversary will have power over them and destroy them."

One of the serious errors made by those in this group is the assumption that being "cleared" by a formal interview actually establishes their standing or worthiness before God. This assumption places unwarranted confidence in formalities and technicalities rather than placing confidence in God. The ultimate formality of returning to God's presence has little to do with passing an interview or with piling up more white marks than black marks in some eternal scorekeeper's book of life. That final formality is not a question of keeping score, but a question of what we have become and what we are.

The development of Christlike character, and the sense of confidence in God that accompanies it, is impossible if our heart is not in it; for it is the nourishing and changing of our heart with which the process is centrally concerned. We cannot have it both ways—drawing near to him with our lips for the limited purpose of looking good or feeling good, but keeping our heart far from him because it is set so much on the things of this world. As Elder Neal A. Maxwell once said, hearts so set must first be broken. Moreover, if we hide our heart from God, we can never give it to him.

If our heart is right, we will be free from the excesses and risks of being either too demanding or not demanding enough with ourselves. The greater our willingness to be humble about our errors and inadequacies, the less we will be likely to repeat them and the more we will learn from our experience. As this attitude draws us closer to God, our confidence in his presence will grow, as will our assurance that we do not seek his face in vain. We might then make the same discovery as did a righteous group of Book of Mormon people: "Nevertheless they did fast and pray oft, and did wax stronger and stronger in their humility, and firmer and firmer in the faith of Christ, unto the filling their souls with joy and consolation, yea, even to the purifying and the sanctification of their hearts, which sanctification cometh because of their yielding their hearts unto God." (Helaman 3:35.)

CHAPTER SEVEN

Human Nature and Learning by Experience

P hilosophers and theologians have argued through the ages about the very nature of man. Surprisingly, a brief review of Western thought shows that the teachings of the restored gospel regarding man's nature contrast remarkably with the dominant views of both the Christian world and the secular society. Yet these gospel teachings also establish a basis for understanding the connection between the Atonement and our need to learn from practical experience.

The teachings of Christian theology since the Middle Ages are rooted in the belief that, through both original sin and natural depravity, man has an inherently evil nature. In both the Catholic and the Protestant traditions, only the grace of God is able to overcome this natural evil. The Catholics have emphasized the place of Church sacraments ("works") in dispensing divine grace, while Protestants have typically believed that God directly bestows grace upon chosen individuals whose religious faith is itself an evidence of the grace they have received. This difference in emphasis is at the heart of the well-worn debates over faith versus works.

Ideas about the corrupt nature of both man and the material world had an enormous influence on early Christian thought and civilization. The art of the medieval era, for example, depicts human beings as flat, insignificant, and shriveled to an almost prune-like state. The heavy religious orientation of the subject matter in medieval art suggests the widely shared assumption that the "other world" of the spirit should be the ultimate focus of man's devotions and aspirations. A similar dichotomy between the material world and the spiritual world is reflected in the most influential writing of the day, typified by St. Augustine's *City of God,* written in the fifth century A.D. Growing out of an intense personal struggle to overcome what he believed to be his own evil nature, Augustine's writings divided both people and human experience into two distinct categories—divine and worldly. For him, the bestowal of undeserved grace was the only escape from the evil of physical pleasures and the influence of the worldly "city of man," leading finally to the heavenly city of God. These ideas laid the foundation for the establishment of monastic orders.

Augustine's thought also had a significant impact a thousand years later on a young Catholic monk named Martin Luther, who had a struggle similar to Augustine's with his own personal temptations. Luther found that the sacraments and other practices administered by the Church brought him no relief from the agony of personal corruption. He then concluded through the scriptural writings of Paul that faith, a gift from God, was the source of mercy and, therefore, justification before God. The gift of faith came not from the Church but from God himself. Thus arose the revolutionary ideas on which much of the Protestant Reformation was based. But even Luther believed that man was evil by nature. He rejected the Greek idea that man can become good through self-improvement.

During Luther's time, another powerful new movement called Humanism arose, in which the Greek heritage came fully to expression. Humanism rejected the medieval view of man. In the Middle Ages, God and the spiritual world had been the center of man's attention. However, to the humanists of the Renaissance, man—not God—was the measure of all things. Believing that man was himself capable of extraordinary accomplishment without divine assistance, the humanists drew heavily on early Greek thought to create the intellectual foundation for an entire series of revolutions stretching over several hundred years in science, politics, art, and virtually every other field. Humanism also influenced Renaissance religion, as new appreciation for the wonders of man's mind and body began to express itself. In the religious art of Michelangelo, for example, human figures took on a majestic and even divine quality, as the shriveled, prune-like forms of Medieval art became full of the human juice of real flesh and blood.

By the time of the European Enlightenment in the eighteenth century, the leading thinkers of the day viewed the natural world not only with sympathy but with fascination, as man's newly awakened rational powers embarked on an adventure of discovery that continues to the present day. A keystone of their thought was the assumption that man was naturally good and, through education and human achievement, perfectible.

Hastened by the optimism and rationalism of the Enlightenment, secularization gradually gained the upper hand over religion and became the driving force behind European and American culture. In the contemporary era even some major elements of Christianity have become more concerned with this world than with the spiritual realms beyond mortality. One symbol of this shift in emphasis was the publication in the 1960s of *The Secular City* by a prominent Protestant theologian, Harvey Cox, who argued that, because of its preoccupation with the world beyond — the world of Augustine's "City of God" — institutional religion had become irrelevant to modern life. Under the influence of similar ideas, many elements of mainstream American Christianity have in recent years devoted increasing attention to improving the human condition in the here and now by focusing primarily on the social and economic environment, especially through movements intended to alleviate poverty and social injustice.

In the midst of this blurring of former distinctions between the religious and secular realms, the idea that the individual person is inherently good has become an implicit assumption

127

shared by most educated Americans, with or without a religious orientation. Such an assumption arises naturally from the modern viewpoint that social problems are primarily the result of environmental shortcomings rather than personal failures. And, of course, environmental factors do influence individual and collective failures, sometimes in overwhelming ways. This viewpoint takes on added strength from the growing perception that the greatest threats to peace and personal freedom come from vast, impersonal forces beyond the control of any individual, such as nuclear war and threats of worldwide economic chaos.

Assumptions that question our level of individual responsibility for our most personal problems have also encouraged a recent popular movement that urges individuals to accept themselves as they are. This movement resists the authority of social institutions and norms that seem either to confine or to change people.[1]

There are, of course, exceptions to this general pattern. Some religious groups have not yet immersed themselves completely in the secular city. They continue to stress the need for personal redemption as the best solution to human misery. Some also still preach the doctrine that man is totally depraved and, hence, totally dependent for salvation upon God's mercy rather than upon one's own actions or achievements. Only a few years ago, I attended the funeral for a Protestant woman who had spent virtually all of her ample wealth in the service of religious, educational, and other charitable causes. After the first speaker praised her for her "Christian attitudes" and her numerous worthy financial contributions, her own minister spoke, scolding the first speaker and anyone else in the funeral congregation who believed her charitable acts would play any role at all in her final judgment before God. He stated that God's decision whether to extend his mercy to her was exclusively in God's hands and her conduct could not influence his choice.

But today's typical educated American probably regards

those who still preach the doctrine of man's inherently evil nature with the same quaint amusement that most Puritans felt toward the severe doctrines of Calvinism within a hundred years after the Puritans first arrived on American soil:

> In these various ways the Puritan philosophy lost its hold on life in New England. The theory of the utter dependence of man on his sovereign God ceased to have any relevance to the facts of Puritan experience. Nevertheless, it was not discarded. The preachers continued to preach it and the laymen continued to hear it; not because either of them believed it, but because they cherished it. Beliefs seldom become doubts; they become ritual. They become intrinsic parts of the social heritage, themes of public celebration. Thus the sense of sin became a genteel tradition, cherished in the imagination long after it had been surrendered in practice. The Puritan insistence on human depravity became the compensatory justification of Yankee moral complacency.[2]

Whatever the actual state of American spiritual life in the modern world, this brief summary of the two major ideas about man's essential nature suggests the historical alternatives to the teachings of the restored gospel. In summary, there are two main alternatives: First, one can assume that man's nature is inherently evil and then take one's pick between (a) the traditional Protestant view of confessing faith in Christ as the source of unmerited grace, and (b) the traditional Catholic belief that the Church's sacraments and rituals are the primary source of otherwise unmerited grace. In both cases, the need for grace is inescapably intertwined with the assumption that man's evil choices are primarily due to his sinful nature rather than the result of his own responsible will.

Second, one can assume that man's nature is inherently good and then take one's pick among an array of competing modern ideas about the best solution to the environmental problems that are believed to cause human misery. Among those who assume that man is inherently good there are many religious and secular alternatives; but they all tend to focus primarily on large-scale social, political, economic, and psychological redemption from the evils of mass society, as distinguished from individual spiritual redemption. Personal redemption seems far less necessary or even helpful if man's nature is already good.

The teachings of The Church of Jesus Christ of Latter-day Saints stand in vivid contrast to both of these major ideas about the nature of man and the process of redemption. When the Lord first instructed Adam that he should be baptized, Adam asked why baptism was necessary. The Lord's answer might strike today's Christian world as a revolutionary statement of theology regarding both original sin and the purpose of experience in mortality:

> And our father Adam spake unto the Lord, and said: Why is it that men must repent and be baptized in water? And the Lord said unto Adam: *Behold I have forgiven thee thy transgression in the Garden of Eden.*
>
> Hence came the saying abroad among the people, that *the Son of God hath atoned for original guilt,* wherein the sins of the parents cannot be answered upon the heads of the children, for they are *whole* from the foundation of the world.
>
> And the Lord spake unto Adam, saying: Inasmuch as thy children are conceived in sin, even so when they begin to grow up, sin conceiveth in their hearts, and *they taste the bitter, that they may know to prize the good.*
>
> And *it is given unto them to know good from evil; wherefore they are agents* unto themselves, and I have given unto you another law and commandment.
>
> *Wherefore,* teach it unto your children, that *all men, everywhere, must repent,* or they can in nowise

inherit the kingdom of God, for no unclean thing
can dwell there.... (Moses 6:53-57; emphasis
added.)

The Lord taught Adam that the Atonement of Christ would
atone for his transgression in the garden. The children of Adam
and Eve were therefore redeemed from the penalties of original sin as a pure act of grace, embodied in the Atonement.
This portion of the Atonement comes as a free gift to all mankind, just as does the Resurrection.

But through the effects of the Fall, Adam's children were
born into a world in which they were subject to temptation,
sin, bitterness, and death. The nature of those born under these
conditions is described in this passage as "*whole* from the
foundation of the world." In modern revelation, the Lord explained further that, "Every spirit of man was *innocent* in the
beginning; and God having redeemed man from the fall, men
became again, in their infant state, *innocent* before God."
(D&C 93:38; emphasis added.) The descriptive terms *whole*
and *innocent* suggest that those who enter the mortal sphere
are at first *neither* good *nor* evil *by nature*.

Those born into such innocence are given the mortal experience that they might learn "to prize the good" through
the exercise of free choice in an environment where both good
and evil are fully available. God seems to have anticipated that
all of us would experience the bitter taste of pain, adversity,
and evil for the express and valuable purpose of giving *meaning* to "the good." Meaning derives from experience. Thus,
some of our experience with evil during our days of mortality
may be purposely intended to make the choice of "good" a
more meaningful choice. As we saw earlier, Lehi's teachings
amplify this possibility:

And now, behold, if Adam had not transgressed
he would not have fallen, but he would have remained in the garden of Eden....
And [Adam and Eve] would have had no children;

131

wherefore they *would have remained in a state of
innocence, having no joy, for they knew no misery;
doing no good, for they knew no sin.*

Adam fell that men might be [mortal], and men
are [mortal], that they might have joy. (2 Nephi 2:22-
23, 25; emphasis added.)

Experienced parents will detect in this statement a connection between having children and knowing misery. But they
will also detect the connection between having children and
knowing joy. It is the context of misery and sin that gives
meaning to both joy and doing good.

We may also see in this statement the reason why the Fall
was a positive rather than a negative chapter in human history.
Adam literally exulted for joy when he began to discover after
the expulsion from Eden the meaning given to his life by that
experience: "Blessed be the name of God, for because of my
transgression my eyes are opened, and in this life I shall have
joy, and again in the flesh shall I see God." (Moses 5:10.)

As explained by Elder John A. Widtsoe, and quoted previously, "These were not the words of sinners or of repentant
sinners."[3] Similarly, the *children* of Adam and Eve who truly
learn of life's meaning from their experiences with opposition
should also be seen in a light different from the one we usually
cast when we think of "sinners." Once we understand that
God gave Adam the right to "choose for thyself, for it is given
unto thee" (Moses 3:17), it becomes more clear that the commandment to not eat of the forbidden fruit was primarily a
warning of the consequences that would follow the choice to
become mortal. But our first parents chose wisely and courageously.

As a result of these events, Adam's children were born in
wholeness or innocence into a mortal experience that can lead
them to understanding and joy. Yet King Benjamin taught his
people that "the natural man is an enemy to God, and has been
from the fall of Adam." (Mosiah 3:19.) Something must happen
to Adam's children to make them "natural men" after they

become accountable for their sins, because we also know that those who die before the age of accountability are sufficiently pure that they are saved in the celestial kingdom. (See Moroni 8.) The way in which some after that age become enemies to God was described by Enoch: "Because that Adam fell, we are; and by his fall came death; and we are made partakers of misery and woe. Behold Satan hath come among the children of men, and tempteth them to worship him; and men have become carnal, sensual, and devilish, and are shut out from the presence of God." (Moses 6:48-49.)

This statement confirms that those who might be called "natural men" are not automatically in that condition because of the Fall, but because — after the Fall — they yield to the temptation given all people to "worship" Satan. To the extent that men or women submit to that invitation, they "become carnal, sensual, and devilish," or, eventually, *evil by nature*, as the result of their own free and unrepented choices. These are they who, like Cain and those who joined him, "loved Satan more than God." (Moses 5:28.) It was because of their influence that "the works of darkness began to prevail among all the sons of men." (Moses 5:55.)

On the other hand, many who "taste the bitter" enough to sense its contrast with "the good" will consciously accept the Lord's atoning grace, willingly repent, and thus learn from their experience to prize the good. These are they who yield "to the enticings of the Holy Spirit, and putteth off the natural man and becometh a saint through the atonement of Christ the Lord." (Mosiah 3:19.) Through the combined effect of their repentance, their efforts to learn, and the spiritual power of the Atonement through the grace of Christ, these children of Adam become "as a child, submissive, meek, humble, patient, full of love." (Mosiah 3:19.) Through the bestowal of Christlike attributes, they can then ultimately become saints or, in other words, *good by nature* — even divine. That is the final potential of the spirit offspring of God, to become as he is.

Thus we see that the children of Adam and Eve have the

133

capacity, in the beginning of their earthly experience, to choose a path that leads toward either a divine or a devilish nature. What they finally become depends significantly on the extent to which they choose one course or the other: "Man could not act for himself save it should be that he was enticed by the one or the other." (2 Nephi 2:16.) That choice places them under the influence of either Satan or Christ, both of whom have power to more fully develop the nature of their followers. The Lorenzo Snow couplet expresses a true statement: "As man is, God once was; and as God is, man may become." But it is also true that as man is, Cain once was; and as Cain is, man may become. As Jacob taught, without the blessings of the Atonement we would not only become "subject to" the devil, but would actually "become devils." (2 Nephi 9:8-9.)

The American philosopher, William James, once asked the question, Is life worth living? He replied, answering his own question, "That depends on the liver." In other words, whether life is worth living depends on who is living it. Similarly, whether man's nature is good or evil depends ultimately on the man, or the woman, and on the divine or satanic influences to which they submit.

When Adam said, "They taste the bitter, that they may know to prize the good," and when Lehi said, "Having no joy, for they knew no misery; doing no good, for they knew no sin," both prophets were expressing the principle that the development of a capacity for autonomous personal action requires real choice. However, as important as is free agency in the abstract, there is more to these prophetic teachings than the general establishment of grounds for free choice. They are also teaching us about *learning from experience*, an idea that helps to explain why God would consciously place us in this risky environment we call mortality. For, as he said in modern revelation, "If they never should have bitter they *could not know the sweet*." (D&C 29:39; emphasis added.)

Human beings learn in two very different ways. Sometimes learning involves such purely intellectual processes as memorizing information or sketching the abstractions of a proper theory. At other times, learning involves the more practical process of skill development, or the *application* of theory. We have noticed in our family, for example, that our children have a much easier time learning the theory of gospel principles than they have putting those ideas into practice. In learning to master any skill, whether playing a musical instrument, fixing an automobile, playing basketball, or running a computer, we learn primarily through a process of trial and error. Knowing the theory somehow does not keep us from making errors. But if we learn from the errors we make in the realm of practice, we make progress.

The process of learning to live the gospel involves both theory and practice. I can imagine that the premortal life was a better environment for learning gospel theory than it was for learning the practical skills of righteousness. Perhaps partly for that very reason, our Father in Heaven created the earth, our bodies, and the opportunity of mortal experience: "We will take of these materials, and we will make an earth whereon these may dwell; and *we will prove them herewith*, to see if they will do all things whatsoever the Lord their God shall command them." (Abraham 3:24-25; emphasis added.) Becoming like our Father necessarily involves a *process* of growth and development. This process requires that we learn capacities and skills, not merely collect information. And there is something about the way we acquire skills and develop qualities of character that requires our participation: We learn to do by doing. To a significant degree, our development of such Christian virtues as patience, unselfishness, and kindness depends upon this skill-development process.

The conditions and experiences necessary for these developmental forms of learning explain a good deal about otherwise puzzling and sometimes very difficult human problems. For one thing, the need for a skill-oriented learning environment helps explain why there is a veil between our world of mortality and God's world of the eternities.[4] This same need underscores the importance of free agency, because "there is something about forcing people to be righteous that interferes with, even prohibits, the process that righteousness in a free environment is designed to enable. Righteous living causes something to happen to people."[5] The nature of skill development also explains, in part, the importance of following as a personal example the Savior's manner of living: "By watching the master and emulating his efforts in the presence of his example, the apprentice unconsciously picks up the rules of the art. . . . These hidden rules can be assimilated only by a person who surrenders himself to that extent uncritically to the imitation of another."[6]

Of course, the tuition is very high in the school of hard knocks. Part of the price we pay for learning through practice is that we face a continual stream of mistakes and errors and missteps. We may learn to prize the good by tasting the bitter, but bitter tastes are by definition unpleasant. Yet by this means we learn to "know good from evil," and we become "agents unto [ourselves]." (Moses 6:56.)

Without both agency and some experience with opposition (experience that includes the mistakes that go with practice), it is not possible to have real learning — or real progress toward life, joy, and meaning.

A young piano student encountered a traumatic stage in her musical development when she began feeling discouraged about making mistakes. It frustrated her that every time she worked through her errors in a piece enough to play it well, her teacher would assign a new piece and she would begin playing wrong notes all over again. She protested in tears to her teacher that, because she kept making mistakes, it was obvious she wasn't learning to play the piano; and she saw no point in continuing to try. The teacher reassured her that nobody in all the world had ever learned to play the piano without making many, many mistakes. Then said the teacher, the students who really learn to play well are those who learn from

136

their mistakes. Those who keep making the same mistakes never do learn to play.

So it is with those who try to learn any other skill, whether typewriting, bicycling, or even learning how to love. There will always be mistakes in each phase of the learning process, from those awkward beginning stages toward the tentativeness of intermediacy and finally the confidence of advanced studies.

Every new husband or new wife has experienced the sharp pains that come in touching the nerves of outer limits, as one seeks to strike the right balance between one's own needs and the needs of one's partner. Most of us also know the feeling of sudden anger, and we have struggled to learn when and how to control it. We can learn much when our anger goes too far and others are hurt. Perhaps we are hurt ourselves. So goes our learning about honesty, as we try to find our way through the gray areas in reporting our time to an employer or our income to the government. Young people in their early romantic relationships learn from experience about physical temptation and will probably sense when they are going a little too far. In the early stages with these commonplace experiences, the warning that we have tasted the bitter often comes only from within our own conscience. If we are even mildly sensitive, we may also see the pained looks on the faces of those we have disappointed or hurt.

The crucial question in these experiences is not whether they will come along, as all of us encounter them; rather, the question is whether we can learn from our early mistakes. If we can, even if only gradually, we will learn to prize the good. Our maturation will be underway. If we cannot, we will move into larger-scale transgressions, and the voice of conscience may grow ever more dim. It may take the experience of a serious transgression for us to sense the importance of learning from a mistake, for sometimes only when we have drunk deeply from the gall of bitterness do we taste it enough to realize what it is.

Whether our experiences are mild or full-blown, the learning process is in effect, and the principle of line upon line, precept upon precept, will apply:

> He that will harden his heart, the same receiveth the lesser portion of the word; and he that will not harden his heart, to him is given the greater portion of the word, until it is given unto him to know the mysteries of God until he know them in full.
>
> And they that will harden their hearts, to them is given the lesser portion of the word until they know nothing concerning his mysteries; and then they are taken captive by the devil, and led by his will down to destruction. Now this is what is meant by the chains of hell. (Alma 12:10-11.)

Some will learn from their errors and accept the Atonement by their repentance and their acknowledgment that the Savior is compensating for their mistakes. Others will not learn and will refuse to accept the Atonement. Through one or the other of these alternatives, the gradual process of becoming either more Christlike or more devilish is underway to some degree for all of us.

Significantly, all of us, including those who learn from the pain of a wounded conscience, need the Savior's help in compensating for the effects of our mistakes as well as our deliberate sins. For that reason Paul could say, "*All* have sinned, and come short of the glory of God." (Romans 3:23; emphasis added.) For that reason the Lord told Adam, "Wherefore teach it unto your children, that *all men, everywhere*, must repent [and be baptized], . . . for no unclean thing can dwell in his presence. . . . " (Moses 6:57; emphasis added.) These statements are true not because of original sin or because all men are inherently evil by nature. They are true because the universal trial-and-error process of learning from experience means all have erred. It is part of the process. The process is good, if we learn from the errors. But learning alone is not enough, for payment must be made to balance the scales of justice after our errors have tipped them toward the negative side. That payment can be made by the Savior's Atonement, through application of the law of mercy, if we but repent by accepting him and by learning to live better through our experience with bitterness.

All this does not mean, of course, that we are justified in going out of our way in the spirit of "all you can eat" from the table of bitterness. As discussed previously, there is no license to sin willfully while planning to repent later. For now, we are considering a basic perspective on all negative human experience, including adversity and inadequacy, miscalculations and carelessness, along with deliberate and willful transgression. All are part of opposition and mortality, and all can be the source of growth and development, depending upon our response to them.

This perspective on our experiences with "the bitter" may sound less harsh than the way some would describe the place of sin and evil. But that is precisely why it is essential to gain the perspective that life is a learning laboratory. Without this understanding, we may miss some of life's most vital lessons, not only about theology but about our relationships with others and our disappointments in ourselves. To err may be human, but our errors do not brand us as inherently evil creatures for whom all is lost; nor are they solely the influence of an external environment for which we have no responsibility. We are free agents and responsible for our errors. But because, after we do all we can, the Atonement cleanses us from the contamination and heals us from the effects of those errors, our mistakes can teach and develop us in ways not otherwise possible. To participate in that process in good faith and with a determination to learn is an important part of "all we can do." The knowledge that our Father lets us taste the bitter precisely so we can prize the good should be a source of courage and good cheer to those who, in their yearning to become like him, seek to do all they can do.

Part II

THE TREE
OF LIFE

CHAPTER EIGHT

Justice, Mercy, and Rehabilitation

Each of the terms *mercy* and *grace* has an independent meaning, but the two words are often used interchangeably, both in these essays and in general discourse among Church members. There may be some value in distinguishing between these terms here, although I do not intend to apply the distinctions rigidly.

Mercy is the more general of the two concepts, having broad enough meaning to include grace within its scope — which is why either term can be used in some contexts to convey the same meaning. Mercy refers both to an attribute of deity and to a universal law that allows a specially qualified third party to pay the penalty of justice on behalf of one who is subject to such a penalty. As one of our Father in Heaven's central attributes (he is a "merciful God"[1]), mercy is in some sense the source of all our blessings — even the blessing of the earth's creation and our very presence here. It is true that the intelligences clothed by our spirits have "no beginning; they existed before, they shall have no end, they shall exist after, for they are gnolaum, or eternal." (Abraham 3:18.) However, this eternal, individual core of each personality was given a spirit body and the opportunity of progress through mortal experience only because of God's loving mercy. "For in him we live, and move, and have our being; . . . For we are also his

143

offspring." (Acts 17:28.) Moreover, that same divine mercy gave us the Atonement, without which there could be no salvation or exaltation — neither hope nor meaning — after this life.

Grace, on the other hand, is the *means* by which mercy enacts many of its miraculous effects, particularly the blessings of the Atonement. Grace is a "divine means of help or strength, given through the bounteous mercy and love of Jesus Christ," and is "made possible by his atoning sacrifice." This "enabling power"[2] is vividly depicted in the Savior's description of himself as the vine on which his faithful followers may be the branches: "I am the vine, ye are the branches: He that abideth in me, and I in him, the same bringeth forth much fruit: for without me ye can do nothing." (John 15:5.)

As discussed previously, the scriptures teach two specific applications of mercy and grace to the process of our personal development. One application is the way the law of mercy allows the Savior's grace to satisfy the law of justice with respect to both (a) Adam's transgression, and (b) our individual sins and inadequacies. A second application of mercy may be seen in the grace-filled bestowal of endowments that perfect and purify us in the process of growing spiritually toward a divine and sanctified nature. Because the first of these applications is more familiar, only a brief review of that doctrine is in order, allowing emphasis in the following three chapters on the role of mercy and grace in the process of sanctification.

The law of justice is an eternal law requiring that whenever a divine commandment is broken there must be a punishment imposed and a compensation made to restore the balance in natural law that was upset by the violation. (See Alma 42.) It is by operation of this law of justice that the punishing effects of both spiritual and physical death act upon mankind.

On the other hand, the positive side of the law of justice assures us that God grants *blessings* to those who *obey* the commandments: "There is a law, irrevocably decreed in heaven before the foundations of this world, upon which all blessings are predicated — and when we obtain any blessing from God, it is by obedience to that law upon which it is predicated." (D&C 130:20-21.) For example, people who care for themselves according to natural laws of health are blessed with stronger physical bodies. Societies that guard against pollution of their environments are blessed by the laws of natural scientific ecology. The laws of natural moral ecology interact in the same way with personal conduct.

Several recognized works of literature illustrate the universal and inherent nature of human responses to violations of the law of justice. Dostoyevsky's *Crime and Punishment*, for example, probes the question whether one who commits a crime as serious as murder could ever be above the law, could ascribe his fault to society, or could otherwise escape legal punishment. As the title of this work suggests, however, Dostoyevsky's main character discovers that he not only cannot escape punishment, but that he must find and accept an adequate punishment to be relieved of an inner torment imposed by human nature itself. Shakespeare's *Macbeth* echoes these ideas. Hawthorne's *The Scarlet Letter* and Tolstoy's *Anna Karenina* explore similar themes in the context of adultery.

The idea of natural law is a controversial topic in modern legal theory, but the underlying concepts of traditional criminal law in Western societies do reflect the idea that some crimes are based on violations of natural law. For example, some crimes are thought to be wrong primarily because they are forbidden by the state. These are *malum prohibitum* acts such as violating a speed limit — wrong because they are prohibited, not necessarily because they are contrary to human nature. However, other crimes, such as murder, have been considered wrong because they are inherently and universally wrong. These acts are *malum in se* — wrong in and of themselves. *Malum in se* crimes are likely to require punishment in many different societies. I cite these references to great literature and to the criminal law only to illustrate that the law of justice is not merely a theological abstraction but has been recognized in other major areas that reflect common human experience.

145

The law of mercy is another eternal law that allows someone other than the transgressor to make the payment required by the law of justice, thereby releasing the transgressor from the obligation to satisfy justice. The operation of the law of mercy is beautifully explained in parable form by Elder Boyd K. Packer in *The Mediator*. Elder Packer describes a debtor who is unable to satisfy his obligation to a demanding creditor. A third-party mediator comes upon the scene and offers to pay the debtor's obligation to the creditor on the debtor's behalf. Both the debtor and the creditor gladly accept this offer, and the debt is satisfied. The creditor and the mediator are then left to work out their relationship on new terms. In this parable the debtor is the individual transgressor; the creditor is the law of justice; and the mediator is the Savior. The law of mercy allows the Atonement to satisfy the law of justice by letting Jesus Christ pay the penalty for our transgressions and for the transgressions of Adam and Eve.

The transgression of Adam and Eve in the Garden of Eden violated the law of justice, thereby subjecting them and all of their children to the penalties of both a physical death and a separation from God, which is sometimes called a spiritual death. If no provision were ever made to overcome the effects of these conditions, we would never be resurrected and would never be able again to enter and remain in the presence of God. The death and resurrection of Christ miraculously have the effect of eliminating the barrier of permanent physical death through a universal resurrection. This is one of the principal blessings of grace through the Atonement: "For since by man came death, by man came also the resurrection of the dead. For as in Adam all die, even so in Christ shall all be made alive." (1 Corinthians 15:21-22.)

In addition, the Atonement compensates for the original transgression of Adam, so that we are responsible only for the spiritual death caused by our own sins and not for that caused by the sin of Adam: "The Son of God hath atoned for original guilt, wherein the sins of the parents cannot be answered upon the heads of the children. . . . " (Moses 6:54.) Thus, the grace of Christ has already atoned for all the effects of Adam's sin *unconditionally* — that is, as a free and unqualified gift that requires no further action on our part.

However, the law of mercy applies to our personal sins only on the condition of our repentance. Our repentance from our sins and our willingness to be baptized and to accept the gospel become the basis for the new obligation between the debtor and the mediator: "But there is a law given, and a punishment affixed, and a repentance granted; which repentance, mercy claimeth; otherwise, justice claimeth the creature and executeth the law, and the law inflicteth the punishment. . . . For behold, justice exerciseth all his demands, and also mercy claimeth all which is her own; and thus, none but the truly penitent are saved." (Alma 42:22, 24.)

All of us are in absolute need of Christ's grace through the law of mercy. Without his atoning sacrifice and his implicit willingness to bear the entire burden of justice, we could not of our own power return permanently to the presence of God, worlds without end.[3] But the sacrifice was made and the law of mercy applies. Death and original sin no longer hold us hostage; and we can obtain forgiveness of our own sins on condition of repentance. Of course, no matter how complete our repentance from our own sins, it would all be to no avail without a Mediator willing to pay our debt to justice in exchange for our repentance. Thus are we utterly dependent on Jesus Christ.

All of us need him, not only because we are the children of Adam, but because to one degree or another, we have all chosen to transgress divine laws in the natural process of tasting the bitter that we may know to prize the good. If we fail to repent, we will be required to face the full penalty of the law of justice. The Savior himself warned: "For behold, I, God, have suffered these things for all, that they might not suffer if they would repent; But if they would not repent they must suffer even as I; which suffering caused myself, even God, the greatest of all, to tremble because of pain, and to bleed at every pore, and to suffer both body and spirit — and would that I might not drink the bitter cup, and shrink." (D&C 19:16-18.)

Suppose some of us do not repent and, as a result, personally satisfy the law of justice by suffering in payment of our own transgressions. Would that place us in the same position with respect to our salvation and exaltation as those whose payment is made by Christ through operation of the law of mercy? If it would, why not lead a sinful life, accept the punishment for it, and still achieve salvation by our own responsibility? These questions lead us to explore the difference between repenting of our sins and paying for them.

Students of criminology and criminal justice tell us that there are several different concepts underlying the public policies that subject lawbreakers to criminal penalties. One pragmatic reason for imprisonment is to protect society by confining those who threaten harm. Another is that giving public visibility to the penalties imposed on lawbreakers may deter others from committing crimes. At a more philosophical level is the theory of *retribution* — the idea that transgressors should "pay" for their sins in the strict sense of the law of justice. Under this theory, lawbreakers should not be released from prison until they have served their allotted time or "paid their debt" to society. Retribution is unconcerned about reforming criminals.

A more modern theory of criminology is *rehabilitation* — the idea that the criminal justice system should have as its primary aim the reform or rehabilitation of offenders. Under this view, the state should do all it can to help prison inmates not merely serve their time but change their lives so they can learn to live in harmony with the laws of society. A commitment to rehabilitative objectives now underlies our system of parole, which seeks the release of those in prison as soon as they can demonstrate their own reform. However, our record in actually achieving rehabilitation among prison inmates has been spotty, in part because the system was not originally created with rehabilitation in mind, and in part because it is so difficult to teach any adult individual to make fundamental changes.

Sadly, the current research on criminology reveals that our society has recently lost confidence in the ideal of rehabilitation. Americans have become unsure not only about whether professional techniques can help a confined person actually change his behavior, but about whether there is any such thing as a normative ideal for personal behavior—that is, any model worth changing toward.[4] Similar doubts may plague the Christian world's view of whether the Atonement really can and does rehabilitate human nature. As Samuel Butler said of America's hypocritical love affair with the New Testament, the people would be equally horrified to hear it doubted *or* to see it practiced.

These various theories of criminal justice may be aptly applied to a consideration of our personal sins. The law of justice requires satisfaction, one way or the other. But if we decline the Savior's invitation to bear the burden of our sins and thus pay the eternal penalty ourselves, we will not have experienced any personal rehabilitation, even if justice is satisfied. We would still, then, be unable to live the laws of the celestial kingdom. Our basic nature would still be whatever it was when we transgressed the law and we became, to that extent, an enemy to God.

The doctrines of grace and repentance are rehabilitative in nature. The great Mediator asks for our repentance *not* because we must "repay" him in exchange for his paying our debt to justice, but because repentance initiates a developmental process that, with the Savior's help, leads us along the path to a saintly character: "For the natural man is an enemy to God, and has been from the fall of Adam, and will be, forever and ever, unless he yields to the enticings of the Holy Spirit, and putteth off the natural man and becometh a saint through the atonement of Christ the Lord, and becometh as a child, submissive, meek, humble, patient, full of love, willing to sub-

149

mit to all things which the Lord seeth fit to inflict upon him, even as a child doth submit to his father." (Mosiah 3:19.)

Thus, paying for our own sins may satisfy justice, but it will not return us to the presence of God. Only the process of change made possible by the combined effects of our repentance and of the Savior's influence in our lives can prepare us to return.

There are two extremes in the perceptions of Church members regarding the process of repentance. Some make it too easy and others make it too hard. In the first category are those who aren't aware of any really big sins in their lives. For them, repentance is a curious abstraction designed for somebody else — most probably for "sinners" involved in major transgressions. They seldom develop much religious intensity, perhaps because they believe that, as children of God, they have relatives in high places who will prevent anything truly damaging from happening to them.

Some others make repentance too easy by looking for shortcuts and easy answers, thinking that quick confessions or breezy apologies alone are enough. Sometimes it is simply too easy just to say I'm sorry. These people should read President Spencer W. Kimball's *The Miracle of Forgiveness,* which reviews a candid, exhaustive, and unsettlingly long list of transgressions, sins of both commission and omission. The book also teaches in masterful depth about the process of repentance. It leaves no doubt that each of us has serious need for continual repentance. Forgiveness is a miracle, but it is not won without our penitent and strenuous effort.

At the other extreme are those for whom the repentance process is not only demanding but overwhelming because it appears to ask more than they possibly know how to give. Many of those in this group somehow have come to believe, perhaps primarily at a subliminal level, that they are fully responsible to compensate for their own sins. Then they discover — hopelessly — that they lack the power to make full compensation by themselves. Such assumptions may spring from an excessively conscientious nature, or they may come from reading too much into gospel teachings that stress man's side of the equation in qualifying for the Savior's mercy. Significantly, these assumptions may also be the result of misunderstanding—perhaps underestimating the power of—the doctrines that teach us of the Savior's mission and Atonement. If the *Newsweek* findings cited previously are any indication, many Church members subscribe to some combination of these erroneous views.

Whatever the reasons, and whatever their numbers, there are many Latter-day Saints who labor under the misapprehension that they must accept not only the *penalties* of justice for their transgressions and inadequacies, but must also assume full responsibility to *compensate* for *all* the *effects* of these acts and shortcomings. Without question, the doctrine of repentance requires that transgressors make the fullest possible restitution for their wrongs, even when doing so may be extremely demanding.[5] But sometimes this expectation cannot be fulfilled. In such cases, those who hold this view are painting themselves into corners of hopeless despair. We not only *do not* compensate fully for all of our own sins, there are times when we *cannot* fully compensate for them.

Suppose a young person is responsible for destroying the virtue of another young person, then desires to repent of his or her wrongdoing. His understanding of repentance moves him to try to make restitution, and there is much he can and should do.[6] But ultimately, he cannot give back virtue the way he would return a stolen car, nor can he see a way to restore his own lost virtue. If he takes seriously his obligation to "make everything right" through repentance, his sense of heavy obligation may finally be his undoing, because he simply lacks the power to restore what is lost. There aren't enough *R*'s in the steps of repentance, not enough power of restoration within the limits of human ability. Because we lack the power to compensate fully for the effects of our transgressions, we are utterly dependent on Christ, no matter how earnest our repentance.

This is not to say that in cases of serious transgression repentance is impossible or that virtue cannot be regained. Such restitution is indeed possible, but only through the Savior's intervention—after all we can do. Until those in such predicaments find the Savior at the heart of the Atonement, as did Alma the Younger, there is no complete escape and no final relief. (See Alma 36.) Once that dawns on us, how exquisite it is to discover that the Divine Redeemer truly will liberate repentant captives from the bondage of sin. Honest transgressors who make this discovery are powerful witnesses about the need for a personal Savior.

Some who carry the burden of serious sin also believe they must somehow "pay" for their mistakes through a Church disciplinary council, feeling that some high level of public shame will make adequate payment. But disciplinary councils do not pay for sins. They are courts of love, not courts of shame. A court may in special cases aid the repentance process by creating a clean slate for those with truly extraordinary problems, but it doesn't have the power to yield a changed heart and a new course of life. And it is assuredly no substitute for the payment Jesus has already made. Repentance in the case of extended transgression is far more difficult than mere public humiliation, but it is the Savior who carries the heaviest burden of sin from such a case—in exchange not merely for shame and public pain, but in exchange for a broken heart and a contrite spirit, and a faithful future course of life. So understood, a Church court is not the last step on the way out of the Church; rather, it can be the first step on the way back.

The Savior's mercy compensates "after all we can do," not only for the consequences of our sins, but also for the harmful consequences of our neglect and poor judgment—or, for that matter, the harmful consequences of decisions that were not in fact so poor to begin with. The feelings of parents whose children go astray are a particularly apt illustration of the need for mercy of this special kind.

I once had a sad and tender conversation with a stake

president whose entire life represented a pattern of stalwart obedience. But he and his equally stalwart wife were carrying the burden of feeling total responsibility for the rebellion of their wayward son. He told me about their boy's very serious mischief and their inability to contain him, despite continual and fervent effort. Then he said, "You know, we always tell our members that no other success can compensate for failure in the home. And the scriptures say that if a man doesn't know how to manage his own house, how shall he take care of the Church?" (See 1 Timothy 3:5.) Because of what he saw as his failure in the home, this man asked if he should request a release from his Church position.

It was impossible for me to know, and probably impossible for him to know, just how much blame was really his for what his son was doing. But I knew firsthand of his good faith, his good heart, his own good life, and the spiritually successful lives of his other children. As I saw the tears in his eyes, I thought of the prophet Alma, whose rebellious son repented and later himself became a prophet. The older Alma was not released from his position as the high priest among the people of Zarahemla. I thought of other parents whose adolescent children have agency and friends and minds of their own. I thought of our Father in Heaven, whose rebellious offspring included not only Satan and Cain, but a third of the hosts of heaven.

I thought also that, while it is true that we can achieve no other success that will in fact compensate for our failures within or outside our homes, there is a success that compensates when we cannot—after all we can do in good faith. That success is the Atonement of Jesus Christ, whose influence can mend what for us is beyond repair. Perhaps, I thought, that holy influence could even do for this man's son what it did for the younger Alma.

Once we do all we can do, thereby qualifying for the blessings of mercy, the law of justice is satisfied. In addition, the Savior's healing power may do its work of compensation.

But restoring the balance of justice and restitution to an even state is not yet enough. Faith, repentance, and baptism are essential, but they are only the beginning, the gate by which we should enter the "strait and narrow path which leads to eternal life" (see 2 Nephi 31:17-18), not the end of the road.

> And now, my beloved brethren, after ye have gotten into this strait and narrow path, I would ask if all is done? Behold, I say unto you, Nay; for ye have not come thus far save it were by the word of Christ with unshaken faith in him, relying wholly upon the merits of him who is mighty to save.
>
> Wherefore, ye must press forward with a stead-fastness in Christ, having a perfect brightness of hope, and a love of God and of all men.... and endure to the end.... (2 Nephi 31:19-20.)

To receive the remaining blessings of the tree of life, we will continue to rely wholly upon the merits of him who is mighty to save.

CHAPTER NINE

Grace and the Higher Law

Ln the previous chapter we reviewed the doctrines of justice and mercy and the process of rehabilitation made possible through repentance and the Atonement. This chapter continues those themes, applying the Savior's grace to the next stage of spiritual development, which extends beyond our satisfying the law of justice. This is the mature stage following baptism and the remission of sins. In this stage, by pressing forward, feasting upon the word of Christ, and enduring to the end (see 2 Nephi 31:20), we may become as Christ is.

Before considering this second stage of spiritual development, two preliminary observations are in order. For one thing, the two-stage process being described here is not necessarily a sequential one. Once we have repented enough to qualify for baptism, that does not mean we will never need the repentance principle again. Our partaking of the sacrament on a weekly basis allows us not only to renew our covenants, but to reaffirm the ongoing process implied by faith, repentance, and baptism. Also in that weekly renewal, the Lord reaffirms his promise to us of continual atonement. This is the process, as King Benjamin called it, of retaining a remission of our sins from day to day. (See Mosiah 4:12, 26.)

In a similar way, the Savior's gift of grace to us is not

necessarily limited in time to "after" all we can do. We may receive his grace before, during, and after the time when we expend our own efforts. Nevertheless, it is helpful to an understanding of the total forgiveness and sanctification process to view the relationship between man's effort and God's grace in two stages.

In addition, stage two is less widely discussed than the more familiar terrain of justice, mercy, and repentance. For that reason, our thoughts on the topic may well be less structured and make use of less familiar terminology than we typically find in discussions of the Atonement that confine themselves to stage one. Still, the general idea that we should move beyond repentance and baptism toward some holier, perfected, or sanctified state is clearly taught in the scriptures. For example, "Therefore not leaving the principles of the doctrine of Christ, let us go on unto perfection; not laying again the foundation of repentance from dead works, and of faith toward God." (JST, Hebrews 6:1.) The scriptures also teach that in this second stage, the Savior's grace has as vital a role to play as in stage one.

Several gospel concepts suggest that there are two stages of spiritual development. One of these is the doctrine of spiritual rebirth, which is taught eloquently in the Book of Mormon. In the preparatory stage, we are born of the water through baptism; in the advanced stage, we are born of the spirit. (See, in particular, Mosiah 5, 27; Alma 5.) We must experience both births to enter the kingdom of heaven. (See John 3:5.)

Another expression of advanced spiritual maturity is the idea of entering into the "rest" of the Lord. The power of the Melchizedek Priesthood has some vital role to play in both preparing and allowing the Saints access to this special state while still in mortality. Moses and the higher priesthood were taken from the children of Israel because the people "hardened their hearts" until the Lord "swore that they should not enter into his *rest* while in the wilderness, *which rest is the fulness of his glory*." (D&C 84:24; emphasis added.)

And Alma taught that the high priests of his day had been called in the premortal life with a "holy calling . . . prepared from the foundation of the world," for the purpose of teaching God's "commandments unto the children of men, that they also might enter into his *rest.*" (See Alma 13:5, 6; emphasis added.) Because of their faithful response to such instruction, "there were many, exceedingly great many, who were made pure and *entered into the rest of the Lord* their God." (Alma 13:12; emphasis added.) (See also Moroni 7:3.)

The scriptures also draw a distinction between the law of Moses and the gospel of Jesus Christ, suggesting that the law of Moses is a preparatory law designed to lead us to the higher law or the fulness of Christ's gospel. A similar distinction is reflected in the "preparatory" role of the "lesser" Aaronic Priesthood, which is ultimately fulfilled in the "greater" Melchizedek Priesthood. (See D&C 84: 18-27.)

Let us consider the general relationship between preparatory and advanced stages through a few illustrations. I once heard someone summarize the "goals" a member of the Church should have: From birth to age eight, the goal is baptism. From age eight to age twelve, the goal is graduating from Primary and, for young men, being ordained to the Aaronic Priesthood. At each interval from ages twelve to fourteen, fourteen to sixteen, and sixteen to eighteen there is an ordination or a class graduation. Between ages eighteen and twenty-five the goals would include a mission, education, and temple marriage. But after age twenty-five, the summary concluded, there is only one goal: to raise and provide for a righteous family and to die faithful. After age twenty-five, he said, there is but one simple age bracket and two simple goals.

I remember wondering aloud to myself as I heard this summary: Is there any sense of progress after age twenty-six? Will I never graduate from the gospel doctrine class? Will I play ward basketball on the "old men's" team forever?

Had I been sketching my impressions of what it means to grow to real maturity in the Church, I would have added more

157

details and some other lifetime goals in that last age bracket. Yet, in an interesting way, this sketch of expectations for personal development suggests to us how the higher law of the gospel of Jesus Christ must have seemed to some of the Jews of Christ's time. Having interpreted and reinterpreted the nuances of the law of Moses for centuries, most Jews were quite unprepared for the broad and lofty principles Jesus taught them. When the lawyer asked Jesus, "Which is the great commandment in the law?" he probably expected a complex answer. But the Lord told him simply, "Thou shalt love the Lord thy God with all thy heart, and with all thy soul, and with all thy mind. This is the first and great commandment. And the second is like unto it, Thou shalt love thy neighbour as thyself. On these two commandments hang all the law and the prophets." (Matthew 22:37-40.)

The gospel of the higher law was so simple and so profound that the Pharisees and other learned people of Christ's day missed it completely. They missed the simple part—the core—and they missed everything.

I have wondered if we, too, might at times suffer from this "blindness" that comes from "looking beyond the mark." (See Jacob 4:14.) Because we face that risk, we must learn what it means for our personal growth in the gospel to move from preparatory levels to the levels of fulfillment; from the letter of the law to the spirit of the law; from an emphasis on externals to an emphasis on the internal; from milk to meat; from the Ten Commandments to the gospel of love. For, on our mature understanding of the higher law hangs "all the law and the prophets"—and all the goals after age twenty-five.

The Lord taught Adam and Eve the fulness of the gospel of Jesus Christ (the higher law), as he did all the prophets until the time of Moses. Enoch and his people, and Abraham, Isaac, and Jacob not only had the fulness of the gospel, but they lived it to the point that some of them have already entered into their exaltation. (See D&C 132:37.) When Moses first went to Mount Sinai while the children of Israel waited below, he was also given the higher law. But because the Israelites "hardened their hearts and could not endure his presence," the Lord replaced the higher law with the Ten Commandments. Then he "took Moses out of their midst, and the Holy [Melchizedek] Priesthood also." (See D&C 84:24-25.)

The Aaronic Priesthood continued with the Israelites until the coming of Christ. During this same era, Israel was governed by a set of laws based on the Ten Commandments. This "preparatory gospel" of the Aaronic Priesthood "is the gospel of repentance and of baptism, and the remission of sins, and the law of carnal commandments." (See D&C 84:26-27.)

Repentance, baptism, and the remission of sins are part of the lesser law. These principles and ordinances are fundamental and even hold "the key of the ministering of angels." (D&C 84:26.) But they are still only the beginning of our spiritual growth. They are but the gate by which we enter the straight and narrow path that leads to eternal life. When we move on to the more mature stage represented by the blessings of the Melchizedek Priesthood and the temple ordinances, we advance to a higher level of religious life.

In his letter to the Hebrews, the Apostle Paul explained to the Jews how the new covenant (also known as the higher law, the fulness of the gospel, and the New Testament) differed from the covenant of the lesser law. He wrote that Christ was "the mediator of a better covenant, which was established upon better promises. For if that first covenant had been faultless, then should no place have been sought for the second." (Hebrews 8:6-7.) The Ten Commandments had been written on tablets of stone and had to be interpreted by Levite priests, who mediated between the people and their God. But the new covenant placed the people in direct contact with Jehovah: "I will put my laws into their mind, and write them in their hearts: and I will be to them a God, and they shall be to me a people: And they shall not teach every man his neighbour, and every man his brother, saying, Know the Lord: for all shall know me, from the least to the greatest." (Hebrews 8:10-11.)

159

The scriptures are soaked through with references to the difference between the two laws, the two covenants, the two priesthoods. Always it is made clear that the preparatory law is to be respected and obeyed, the temporal or "carnal commandments" followed: "Woe unto you, scribes and Pharisees, hypocrites! for ye pay tithe of mint and anise and cummin, and have omitted the weightier matters of the law, judgment, mercy, and faith: These ought ye to have done, *and not to leave the other undone*. Ye blind guides, which strain at a gnat, and swallow a camel." (Matthew 23:23-24.)

The higher law does not replace the lower law—it supplements and fulfills it. Nephi understood this: "We keep the law of Moses, and look forward with steadfastness unto Christ, until the law shall be fulfilled. For, for this end was the law given; wherefore the law hath become dead unto us, and we are made alive in Christ because of our faith; yet we keep the law because of the commandments." (2 Nephi 25:24-25.)

Yet Nephi also candidly acknowledged that "we speak concerning the law [of Moses] that our children may know the deadness of the law; and they, by knowing the deadness of the law, may look forward unto that life which is in Christ, and know for what end the law was given." (2 Nephi 25:27.)

Amplifying the theme of the law's "deadness," Paul tells us that "the letter killeth, but the spirit giveth life." (2 Corinthians 3:6.) For the "epistle of Christ" (the higher law) is given to us "not with ink, but with the Spirit of the living God; not in tables of stone [as the law of Moses was given], but in fleshy tables of the heart." (2 Corinthians 3:3.)

Still, the lower law has the important purpose of being "our schoolmaster to bring us unto Christ." (Galatians 3:24.) And once the schoolmaster of the lower law brings us to Christ, he himself becomes the source of the higher law as it applies to our personal needs. "Wherefore . . . feast upon the words of Christ; for behold, the words of Christ will tell you all things what ye should do." (2 Nephi 32:3.) As he taught the Nephites: "The law . . . given unto Moses hath an end in me. Behold, *I am the law*, and the light. Look unto me, and endure to the end, and ye shall live. . . . " (See 3 Nephi 15:8-9.)

This scriptural context can illuminate our attempts to live the gospel in its fullest sense, for without an understanding of what is expected of us after we have been prepared by the lower law, we could be adrift on a plateau of complacency during much of our adult lives. Without some breakthrough in attitude that lifts us to the plane of the higher law, we may think of living the gospel as little more than a superficial adherence to external commandments. At that limited level, we may not even recognize the Savior when he comes into our lives hoping to lead us beyond the schoolmaster that brought us to him.

As a practical matter, how is the higher law different? Is it simply more commandments? On the contrary, it is probably fewer commandments, but commandments of a different quality from the Ten Commandments — wide enough to include the lesser law, deep enough to transcend it. Christ himself made the contrast very vivid in comparing what had been said "by them of old time" with what he expected under the new covenant. The Lord commanded Moses in the Ten Commandments, "Thou shalt not kill." But the higher law requires, "Whosoever is angry with his brother shall be in danger of his judgment." (3 Nephi 12:22.) The Ten Commandments state, "Thou shalt have no other gods before me." But the higher law is more affirmative: "Thou shalt love the Lord thy God with all thy heart, and with all thy soul, and with all thy mind." (Matthew 22:37.)

The contrast between the old covenant and the new covenant is also made plain in the Lord's language to Joseph Smith at the time he gave the Saints "the law of the Church" in 1831. He repeated many of the Ten Commandments, but in a context making clear that the Restoration was based on the higher law — not just the lower law. Consider, in contrast to "thou shalt not commit adultery" in the lower law, this stirring and affirmative new perspective: "Thou shalt love thy wife with all thy heart, and shalt cleave unto her and none else. And he that looketh upon a woman to lust after her shall deny the faith, and shall not have the Spirit; and if he repents not he shall be cast out." (D&C 42:22-23.)

Moses and other Israelite leaders at times tried to teach the broad, positive doctrine of the higher law,[1] but over time the lower law tended to emphasize negative restrictions on conduct—have no other gods, do not commit adultery. This emphasis is less concerned with motive or purpose, less demanding that we *do* anything affirmative, much less *be* anything that extends beyond what we are. The contrast with the higher law is staggering: "*Love thy wife* with all thy heart"; and "*Be* ye therefore perfect. (Matthew 5:48.) The higher law asks not only for new behavior; it asks for a new heart.

Suppose an elder is literally "picked up" by his home teachers on Sunday morning—right out of bed, without waking him. They take him gently to priesthood meeting and place him on a chair without disturbing his slumber. He sleeps right through the meeting, and they take him home. Should the quorum secretary mark him present? If not, how should he record the attendance of the other quorum members who came on their own power but also slept through the meeting? Under the lower law, it is probably enough just to be there. Under the higher law, it is not enough.

Suppose a couple is married in the temple. Is that a "celestial" marriage? Not yet. The letter of the law has been satisfied, but the spirit of the law will wait to see if the partners to the marriage truly become "eternal"—which means, like God. Then the marriage is an "eternal" one—when its partners love as God does, a love not only for each other but for others, and for him.

Yet many of us continue to have a "Ten Commandments" mentality about living the gospel. Most of us have heard those discussions about what one of our children once called "breaking the Sabbath day holy." After hearing a heated exchange about what kind of picnic would be in keeping with the commandment to honor the Sabbath day, I thought to myself that the only safe rule of Sabbath day observance seems to be: You can do anything you want to, as long as you don't have a good time. Instead of focusing so much on what we can't do on Sunday, we need to look at what we can do—even what we get to do on this special day. It is a day of doing, serving, and living joyously—not just a day of naps and don'ts. "The sabbath was made for man, and not man for the sabbath." (Mark 2:27.)

As I think about dress and grooming standards at our Church colleges and university, I yearn for the day when our students will understand the purpose behind the standards, which is so different from merely yielding to them with a technical, superficial compliance. In the mostly Mormon town where I grew up, we held dances in a Church recreation hall on Friday nights and dances in the local National Guard armory on Saturday nights. Many of the same people came—the same partners, the same dance band. But those attending the dances were expected to dress and act more appropriately in the Church building. The message I got was to respect the building; dress and act as you please, as long as you're not on Church property.

Speaking from the perspective of the higher law, the Lord said, "It is not meet that I should command in all things; for he that is compelled in all things, the same is a slothful and not a wise servant." (D&C 58:26.) Those who attend Ricks and BYU may only comply with the outward appearance of dress and grooming standards, but I hope they will also learn enough from those standards about modesty, dignity, masculinity and femininity that as time goes on they will apply those principles sensibly throughout their lives, no longer needing a Church-sponsored code to tell them how to dress. When we learn correct principles, we do govern ourselves.

The Savior gave us the sum and substance of the higher law in the Sermon on the Mount when he taught the doctrine of becoming as he is. Our knowledge of human imperfections—especially our own—makes the goal of perfection seem preposterous. Our inability to control our tongues, our tempers, and our thoughts makes an honest person squirm and a truly perceptive person despair when we talk of living a higher law. To talk about establishing a perfect compliance with temporal, external commandments such as tithing and Church attendance may seem at first blush to be encouraging. But the distance from that point to really having a Christlike heart is overwhelming.

To be overwhelmed with the injunction to be perfect is the right attitude, because it puts us in the frame of mind to realize that we cannot, by ourselves, become as Christ is. With that perspective we are ready to consider the role of grace in the process of becoming perfected.

Jesus taught that we should be perfect as he is perfect. (See 3 Nephi 12:48.) His experience suggests that his own developmental process was marked by his being a recipient of the Father's divine grace. His experience also shows that being free from sin is not the same thing as attaining a state of perfection.

We know that Jesus Christ was the only being ever to have lived in mortality without committing sin. He was without blemish or spot, which qualified him to accept the great sacrifice of carrying the blemishes and sins of all mankind. Yet Christ tasted of a central purpose of mortality by learning and growing through his earthly experience, even though he was without sin:

> Who in the days of his flesh, when he had offered
> up prayers and supplications with strong crying and
> tears unto him that was able to save him from death,
> and was heard in that he feared;
> Though he were a Son, yet learned he obedience
> by the things which he suffered;
> And *being made perfect*, he became the author
> of eternal salvation unto all them that obey him.
> (Hebrews 5:7-9; emphasis added.)

The Savior also received the blessing of his Father's grace

along his path toward attaining the Father's "fulness." He offers us the blessing of following the same path, establishing a relationship with him that mirrors his relationship with the Father:

> And I, John, saw that he received not of the fulness at the first, but received grace for grace;
>
> And he received not of the fulness at first, but continued from grace to grace, until he received a fulness;
>
> And thus was he called the Son of God, because he received not of the fulness at the first.
>
> And I, John, bear record that he received a fulness of the glory of the Father;
>
> And he received all power, both in heaven and on earth, and the glory of the Father was with him, for he dwelt in him.
>
> I give unto you these sayings that you may understand and know how to worship, and know what you worship, that you may come unto the Father in my name, and in due time receive of his fulness.
>
> For if you keep my commandments you shall receive of his fulness, and be glorified in me as I am in the Father; therefore, I say unto you, you shall receive grace for grace. (D&C 93:12-14, 16-17, 19-20.)

Once the law of justice is satisfied and our sins are forgiven, we are then, like the sinless Christ, ready to move forward toward receiving the fulness of the Father by a process of grace.

Other revelations describe this process as part of what it means to be sufficiently perfected to enter the celestial kingdom. In the grand revelation on the three degrees of glory given to Joseph Smith and Sidney Rigdon in 1832, we find this language in the description of the celestial world and those who will inhabit it:

> They are they into whose hands the Father has given all things—

They are they who are priests and kings, *who have received of his fulness,* and of his glory....

These are they who are *just men made perfect* through Jesus the mediator of the new covenant, who wrought out *this perfect atonement* through the shedding of his own blood. (D&C 76:55-56, 69; emphasis added.)

Note the reference to the "fulness" here. Section 93 also mentioned this concept as what Christ received, not at first, but after he had continued, grace for grace. This same fulness was there promised "in due time" to the followers of Christ. Note also that section 76 does not describe those who inherit the celestial kingdom as having attained perfection on their own, but as "just" men who are "made perfect" through some process connected with the Atonement.

We may become "just" or justified (as when a printer lines up the edges of crooked margins; when all the lines are straight, the printing is "justified") when we demonstrate sufficient repentance to receive the Savior's mercy. The demands of justice are then satisfied. This may be the *"justification* through the grace of our Lord and Savior Jesus Christ," which "is just and true." (D&C 20:30.) Then, as a second stage, we may be "made perfect" or sanctified (in addition to receiving forgiveness of our sins) as a further manifestation of the Savior's mercy: "And we know also, that *sanctification* through the grace of our Lord and Savior Jesus Christ is just and true, to all those who love and serve God with all their mights, minds, and strength." (D&C 20:31.) Sanctification is thus the process by which we become holy following baptism.

These passages bear a striking similarity to the final benediction of Moroni at the end of the Book of Mormon, in which the invitation to become perfect through the grace and Atonement of Christ is stated with sublime power. The significance of this description of the second stage of spiritual development is underscored by the realization that Moroni was consciously uttering his final, urgent plea to all mankind, after all else that he and his forebears had written throughout the entire book:

> Yea, come unto Christ, and be perfected in him, and deny yourselves of all ungodliness; and if ye shall deny yourselves of all ungodliness, and love God with all your might, mind, and strength, then is his grace sufficient for you, that by his grace ye may be perfect in Christ; and if by the grace of God ye are perfect in Christ, ye can in nowise deny the power of God.
>
> And again, if ye by the grace of God are perfect in Christ, and deny not his power, then are ye sanctified in Christ by the grace of God, through the shedding of the blood of Christ, which is in the covenant of the Father unto the remission of your sins, that he become holy, without spot. And now I bid unto all, farewell. . . . (Moroni 10:32-34.)

It is natural to wonder just what this process of sanctification means, as a practical matter, and whether it takes on any actual reality during our mortal experience. Our understanding of such a profound idea is necessarily limited by our lack of experience and by the intimate, spiritual nature of the process itself. Nevertheless, we do know that we do not sanctify ourselves solely through our own power. That crucial insight underscores our complete dependence on the Savior. It also relieves us of the impossible burden of constantly failing to achieve by our own exertion the ideal standard of spiritual living to which we are committed by accepting his injunction, "I would that ye should be perfect even as I, or your Father who is in heaven is perfect." (3 Nephi 12:48.)

Indeed, one of the specific expressions of sanctifying grace in mortality is the spiritual endowment of "hope," which grants us a new inner sight that allows us to cope with our natural imperfections with a sense of serenity and optimism.[2]

Other specific manifestations in mortality of the perfecting grace of Christ in the process of sanctification include the gift

167

of charity,[3] the overcoming of evil desires, and the blessings of peace and understanding. The Prophet Mormon beautifully described these purifying endowments and placed them in relationship to our earlier stage of spiritual development:

> And the first fruits of repentance is baptism; and baptism cometh by faith unto the fulfilling the commandments; and the fulfilling the commandments bringeth remission of sins;
> And the remission of sins bringeth meekness, and lowliness of heart; and because of meekness and lowliness of heart cometh the visitation of the Holy Ghost, which Comforter filleth with hope and perfect love, which love endureth by diligence unto prayer, until the end shall come, when all the saints shall dwell with God. (Moroni 8:25-26.)

If such marvelous spiritual power is available to us in the here and now of everyday life, and if we are not expected to achieve actual perfection by ourselves, it is both natural and important to ask, By what standard must we live to qualify for the perfecting power of such grace? We are not likely to find a mechanical list of three or four steps to success in a doctrinal area of such substance that must also be adapted to our individual circumstances. But a few things seem clear. One is that the Lord will probably be most concerned with our core internal attitude of sacrifice — whether our hearts are broken and our spirits contrite.

More specifically, a variety of scriptural passages together suggest a pattern that describes the way we must live in order to prove worthy of the sanctifying gifts. These phrases suggest, as much as anything, a general flavor and feeling:

> Pray unto the Father with all the energy of heart, that ye may be *filled* with this love [charity], which he hath bestowed upon *all who are true followers of his Son,* Jesus Christ.... (Moroni 7:48; emphasis added.)

168

I would speak unto you that are . . . the *peaceable followers of Christ,* and that have obtained a sufficient *hope* by which ye can enter into *the rest of the Lord. . . .*

I judge these things of you *because of your peaceable walk with the children of men.* (Moroni 7:3-4; emphasis added.)

Teach them to *never be weary of good works,* but to be *meek and lowly in heart;* for such shall find rest to their souls. (Alma 37:34; emphasis added.)

See that ye *bridle all your passions,* that ye may be *filled with love.* (Alma 38:12; emphasis added.) [Note the difference between *bridling* and *eliminating* passions; also that being "filled with love" suggests an endowment from outside oneself, such as charity.]

Yea, come unto Christ, and be perfected in him, and *deny yourselves of all ungodliness . . .* and *love God with all your might, mind, and strength,* then is his grace sufficient for you. . . . (Moroni 10:32; emphasis added.)

Because of *meekness and lowliness of heart* cometh the visitation of the Holy Ghost, which . . . *filleth* with hope and perfect love, which love endureth by *diligence unto prayer. . . .* (Moroni 8:26; emphasis added.)

These are they who are *just men made* perfect. . . . (D&C 76:69.)

He *yields to the enticings of the Holy Spirit . . .* and becometh as a child, *submissive, meek, humble, patient, full of love, willing to submit* to all things which the Lord seeth fit to inflict upon him, even *as a child* doth submit to his father. (Mosiah 3:19; emphasis added.)

> And we know also, that sanctification *through the grace* of our Lord and Savior Jesus Christ is just and true, to *all those who love and serve God with all their mights, minds, and strength.* (D&C 20:31; emphasis added.)

> They did *fast and pray* oft, and did wax stronger and stronger in their humility, and firmer and firmer in *the faith of Christ,* unto the *filling* their souls with joy and consolation, yea, even to the purifying and the sanctification of their hearts, which sanctification cometh *because of their yielding their hearts unto God.* (Helaman 3:35; emphasis added.)

These edifying and stirring ideas speak for themselves. It may be worth noting, however, that this is not just another list of virtues; rather, in each case, the author was describing the personal characteristics we must exhibit if we would qualify to receive such specific second-stage endowments and attributes as charity, hope, the rest of the Lord, perfection and sanctification.

There is a significant distinction between (a) the way we must live to qualify for receiving the purifying manifestations of grace, and (b) the qualities that actually characterize those who have received such sanctification. The passages quoted above describe qualities that are very demanding but are still within the reach of our own efforts—being meek and lowly, bridling our passions, denying ourselves of ungodliness, being humble and submissive, loving the Lord to the full extent of *our* own limited might and strength, and humbly offering him our broken heart in the sacrificial attitude of a contrite spirit. These are not descriptions of achieved perfection—which is one reason it is so encouraging to read them.

However, other well-known passages of scripture are far more demanding, because they do read like descriptions of achieved perfection. If read with the assumption that we, by our own effort, should be living in just that way, these passages can be a source of confusion and discouragement. Perhaps these more exacting standards are not a list of ever-more demanding commandments we are expected to master through our own discipline and volition, but are a description of what we will be like when we do receive the full perfecting power of Christ in our lives.

Christ's Sermon on the Mount, for example, sets the lofty standard of forbidding anger and evil thoughts. He also asks us to love our enemies and states that whatever we ask in faith will be given to us. He concludes with the commandment to "be ye therefore perfect." (See Matthew 5:48.) These expectations, desirable as they are, extend past our present reach. Indeed, they extend markedly beyond the level of worthiness necessary to warrant perfecting blessings of additional capacity from outside ourselves. Yet this sermon was such a vital part of the gospel's doctrinal foundation that the Savior taught it to the Nephites among his first words to them.

In the Book of Mormon version of the Sermon on the Mount, Jesus prefaced his teachings with a stirring invitation for the Nephites to accept the gospel — to "come down into the depths of humility and be baptized," for they would then be "visited with fire and with the Holy Ghost, and [would] receive a remission of their sins." (3 Nephi 12:2.)

This preface in the Book of Mormon account is tied to some phrases in the Beatitudes that significantly expand the meaning of some oft-quoted language. For instance, "Blessed are the poor in spirit *who come unto me,* for theirs is the kingdom of heaven." (3 Nephi 12:3.) *Who come unto me* is not present in the version in Matthew, nor is the preface that issues the invitation to come unto him by accepting the fulness of the gospel, including all the blessings bestowed by the Holy Ghost. Moroni described those blessings as including "the visitation of the Holy Ghost, which Comforter filleth with hope and perfect love." (Moroni 8:26.) In other words, the Holy

171

Ghost is the agent by which the sanctifying power of heavenly endowments is administered.

The Sermon on the Mount, as clarified in 3 Nephi, seems to describe what happens when we make all the effort required to repent and serve God to the full extent of our ability and, as a result, are purified and perfected by a power not our own. In that light this sermon is not a statement of unrealistic demands, but a picture of what the Savior's true followers will become through his endowment of grace. It is thus a summary of both stage one and stage two, the preparatory gospel of repentance and baptism, plus the fulness of "the power of godliness" (D&C 84:20) bestowed through operation of the higher law.

A similar illustration is King Benjamin's final discourse to his people. When we read some of the passages in this discourse, we might logically assume that King Benjamin was primarily asking his people to live by an exceedingly high standard:

> And ye will not have a mind to injure one another, but to live peaceably, and to render to every man according to that which is his due.
> And ye will not suffer your children that they . . . transgress the laws of God, and fight and quarrel one with another. . . .
> And . . . ye . . . will succor those that stand in need of your succor. (Mosiah 4:13-14, 16.)
>
> We have no more disposition to do evil, but to do good continually. (Mosiah 5:2.)

In the larger context of his entire sermon, a different perspective emerges. King Benjamin concluded his original address with a powerful statement on the Atonement and a plea that his people take him seriously. After he had concluded, the people were so receptive that a strong spiritual witness came over them, filling them with joy and a remission of their sins. They desired to receive both forgiveness of their sins and the

172

perfecting power of sanctification: "O have mercy, and apply the atoning blood of Christ that we may receive forgiveness of our sins, and our hearts may be purified."(Mosiah 4:2.)

Benjamin then seized this teaching moment to explain further what his people must do if they wished to retain this remission of their sins and continue tasting the love of God that was then upon them. He then gave them counsel which, if followed, would always cause them to "rejoice and be filled with the love of God" and to "grow in the knowledge . . . of that which is just and true." (Mosiah 4:12.) This counsel included his admonition that his people *always* remember the "greatness of God" and their "own nothingness," that they humble themselves in daily prayer, and that they stand "steadfastly in the faith." (Mosiah 4:11.) If the people did these things *after* first receiving a remission of their sins, *then* they would be so filled with the sanctifying power of God's love (charity) that they would, as a direct result, "not have a mind to injure one another," "live peaceably," and so on.

In other words, as we become affirmatively purified and perfected—beyond having achieved remission of our sins— our hearts and minds begin to change, for our very nature is changing.

It was this taste of the divinely bestowed power of godliness that then caused Benjamin's people to say, "The Spirit of the Lord Omnipotent . . . has wrought a mighty change in us, or in our hearts, that we have no more disposition to do evil, but to do good continually." (Mosiah 5:2.)

Perhaps they experienced the rebirth of the Spirit, and King Benjamin counseled them then to seek a course of growth leading from spiritual rebirth to full spiritual maturity. That is the nature of stage two, as we grow from grace to grace, beyond a remission of sins and beyond rebirth until we have been perfected unto receiving the same fulness that Christ himself received from the Father. That fulness is the endowment of a perfected divine nature—being therefore perfect, even as the Father and the Son are perfect. It is the fruit of the tree of life.

CHAPTER TEN

Hope

T he sanctifying grace of the Savior Jesus Christ is the source of an entire cluster of blessings and powers. The Atonement not only atones for our sins and compensates for our inadequacies, it is also the source of spiritual endowments that develop and ultimately transform our very nature.

The agent by which many of these forces enter our lives is the Holy Ghost, that "Comforter" whose "visitation" "filleth with hope and perfect love" — or hope and charity. (Moroni 8:26.) It is "by the reception of the Holy Ghost" that "ye may be sanctified," following repentance and baptism. (3 Nephi 27:20.)

Some manifestations of this sanctifying process may reflect the Holy Ghost's mission to act as a comforter, to bear witness of the Father and the Son, and to "teach you all things, and bring all things to your remembrance." (John 14:26.) The gift of the Holy Ghost thus goes well beyond a right to divine inspiration and guidance. It is by the Holy Ghost that we receive access to certain gifts of the Spirit, many of which are enumerated in D&C 46 — such as the gift of knowing "that Jesus Christ is the Son of God." (D&C 46:13.) Further evidence of the Holy Ghost's influence may be found through the "fruit of the Spirit" — "love, joy, peace, longsuffering, gentleness, goodness, faith, meekness, temperance." (Galatians 5:22-23.) As with other gifts involved in the bestowal of grace toward perfection, the gifts of the Spirit are not given only to those who are themselves perfect; rather, they "are given for the benefit of those who love me and keep all my commandments, *and him that seeketh so to do. . . .*" (D&C 46:9; emphasis added.)

Rather than developing an encyclopedic summary of the various spiritual endowments we may receive through the process of sanctification, I will select for discussion in this and the subsequent chapter only two; yet these two may be at once the most practical and the most profound of the blessings of holiness: hope and charity.

The subject of hope will be treated here in practical terms, in part because hope is such a terribly practical need. The scriptures that refer to "a hope in Christ" (see, for example, Jacob 2:19) may be referring to a particular theological meaning or experience. In a more general sense, hope that derives from our sure conviction of faith in Christ is also a gift of grace that can bestow a spiritual but practical form of the peace and insight necessary to cope patiently with our own sense of personal inadequacy. Along the pathway toward perfection, few obstacles are quite as discouraging as our own awareness that perfection seems a tauntingly unattainable ideal.

No small part of this volume's purpose is to urge the theological reality that the Savior desires to save us from our inadequacies and disappointments as well as from our sins. In the preceding chapters, we have seen these manifestations of "the bitter" take many forms — opposition in all things, psychic pains, growing pains, and life circumstances that continually fall short of excellence. It is in the midst of those very experiences that the arm of the Lord is most likely to be revealed to us in a personal way, as his outstretched hand represents hope in its most meaningful sense.

There always seems to be some distance — let us call it "the gap" — between the real and the ideal; between what is and what ought to be. Let us imagine two circles, one inside the other. The inner boundary is the real, or what is. The outer boundary is the ideal, or what ought to be. We stand at the inner boundary, reaching out, trying to pull reality closer to the lofty ideals to which we have committed ourselves. We are likely to become aware of the distance between these two boundaries when we realize that some things about ourselves are not what we wish they were, or what they ought to be. As that realization grows, so can our level of frustration.

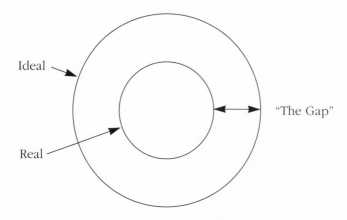

We learn about the gap in a variety of ways. When children gradually become conscious of the imperfections of their parents, the gap may challenge their ability to follow their parents' advice without following their example. New members of the Church learn about the gap when they discover that their seasoned brothers and sisters in the gospel may not always live as Latter-day Saints should live. New missionaries are especially likely to encounter the gap, because they often begin their missionary service with more idealistic commitments than they have ever made before. Yet in spite of their most valiant efforts, they may find themselves fighting back the tears of disappointment when the promised fruits of a positive mental attitude somehow elude them. A hopeful young athlete may dedicate himself to a demanding training program on the assumption that he can achieve whatever he works hard enough to achieve, only to discover he may not be tall enough or talented enough to compete successfully.

At a more personal and spiritual level, perhaps an important prayer goes too long unanswered. Perhaps one suffers some major setback with health, employment, or a marriage prospect, and the heavens do not yield relief. Or suppose one makes solemn commitments to control an anxious tongue or a hair-trigger temper, only to find the tongue or the temper suddenly out of control again. More difficult may be the case of one who repents of some clearly sinful act, even to the point of confessing to a bishop, then commits the same act again. The gap is never more excruciating than in the unguarded moment when a previously forsaken transgression is repeated.

The gap may seem to become a pervasive, ever-present kind of thing. Some mothers dread family-oriented lessons in Relief Society, because emphasizing again the ideals of motherhood can be such a painful reminder of the way one's own circumstances fall short of the ideal. One woman I know told of coming home from such a discussion at a Church gathering, full of new idealism and determination to make hers into the perfect LDS home. As she opened the front door, however, she discovered the tell-tale signs of an imperfect home: the back door left open, the clutter of dirty clothes and toys in bedrooms where order had at last glance prevailed, cold cereal strewn from one end of the family room to the other, and the cat on the kitchen counter eating the lunch meat. That day she thought about the gap.

Then there are the family home evenings and scripture study sessions in our home. Somehow it has not been altogether natural for our children to glide reverently into their places all at once and all on time, prepared to ponder thoughtfully the wonders of eternity. More than likely, especially when they were young, they seemed to come swinging into the family room on the chandeliers like Tarzan on the vines, then would stand on their heads or flip themselves over the back of the couch during most of the lesson. During that stage of our family's history, our bishop lovingly referred to our children as curtain climbers, rug rats, and house apes. There were times in those days when the gap yawned as wide as the Grand Canyon.

But there were also rare moments when, somehow, the gap almost seemed to close. I think, for instance, of the evening an elderly non-Mormon gentleman joined us for home evening as part of his visit to the Ricks College campus. Perhaps his presence affected our children, but whatever the reason, there was something very open and warm and even tender that night in the communication among our young children and the three adults. Some years later, the man who was our guest recalled for me that evening in our home. He had no children of his own but had always dreamed of a pleasant family life with a house full of little ones. He described his evening with our ordinary, lovable, and usually noisy children as one of the sweetest experiences of his adult life.

I also recall the first night we showed the "family slide show," the funniest and most beautiful of our vast collection of pictures of our children, shown at family night with two projectors and individually chosen background music for each member of the family. That was the week before our oldest son left for his mission. We laughed and remembered and enjoyed being together. As we knelt in prayer at the end, there were no curtain climbers or rug rats; just young men and women whose love for one another was dawning on them. The gap seemed very narrow. Still, almost all the time, the gap remains.

After we have experienced the discomfort, the frustration, and even the anguish caused by this gap, we naturally wonder what to do about it. One popular approach is to relieve the tension by simply erasing the outer circle. For example, some call it hypocrisy to claim allegiance to values or ideals that seem unrealistic to attain. To them, the failure of a Latter-day Saint to live up to his professed standards proves a kind of dishonesty equal to or worse than the sins his standards condemn. By implication, then, the standards themselves are called into question. Honesty alone becomes a more admirable standard in this view, because of the rugged integrity that seems to come from modest claims and the total absence of pretense. If you can't practice what you preach, the reasoning goes, then preach what you practice. It is more virtuous to be true to what you claim than it is to claim what is true.

Others who erase the outer circle are trying to remove the discomfort of the gap because it has created negative feelings of guilt. To them, the elimination of guilt is by itself a worthy goal, simply because the guilt-free life seems to make people feel better about themselves. Reflecting this assumption, a therapist who claims to reflect mainstream attitudes among modern psychotherapists wrote in a professional journal that most people in his field believe that being seriously religious "is significantly correlated with emotional disturbance." He continued, "People largely disturb themselves by believing strongly in absolutistic shoulds, oughts, and musts, and most people who dogmatically believe in some religion believe in these health-sabotaging absolutes. . . . The less religious [people] are, the more emotionally healthy they will tend to be."[1] This psychologist further believes that "unequivocal and eternal fidelity or loyalty to any interpersonal commitment, especially marriage," can also "lead to harmful [psychic] consequences," presumably because such commitments are characterized by "absolutistic shoulds, oughts, and musts" of the kind represented by the outer circle of the ideal.

The simple act of erasing the outer circle has a tantalizing power to eliminate frustration and apparent unhappiness, because in one stroke that act eliminates both guilt and the gap. If you are a student and don't like school, if you are a parent who doesn't like caring for children, if you are made uncomfortable by restraining your sexual urges, then (the reasoning goes) accept the liberation of just being honest about yourself. Accept yourself for what you are. It's unnatural to try to be someone you're not. Maybe you're just not celestial material; somebody has to be in those other kingdoms. As one well-known host of a children's television show puts it, "I like you just the way you are."

This line of thought begins with an important truth: We must start where we are and be honest and accepting toward ourselves. But in the popular, breezy form in which this valuable beginning point loses its sense of restraint, pop psychology has captured the American imagination with the misleading idea that self-acceptance is the end of therapeutic or personal development rather than the beginning. Counseling can in this way become less concerned with assisting people toward change and more concerned with simply helping them to be comfortable.[2] That might be an adequate approach for helping someone come to terms with having a terminal illness; but it is unlikely to succeed as well in aiding the processes of personal growth and development.

So understood, a preoccupation with self-acceptance alone can limit our possibilities for growth and change, restrict the power of repentance, and, in effect, deny the Atonement. President McKay occasionally quoted a writer named Beverly Nichols, who wrote that if we deny the possibility of changing human nature, we are in effect saying to the Savior, go back, we don't want you; we don't believe you.

Suppose someone has acknowledged a transgression or a weakness and has fought his way back successfully—only to be confronted again with the same temptation. There is nothing the Evil One would rather have such a person believe than the idea that, "You haven't really changed. You never did. You're not one of those straight arrows—you never were. So why don't you quit kidding yourself? The leopard cannot change his spots."

We do not become perfect in one great act, just as we do not become irreversibly evil in one great act—or two. But painfully, slowly, it really is possible to push the inner circle toward the ideal. To trust the Savior's power in this matter is at the very heart of the gospel's purpose—to make bad men good and good men better.

Some people have quite another problem with the gap. They eliminate the tension and frustration the gap causes by erasing the inner circle of reality. Such people cling to the ideal so single-mindedly that they are able to avoid the pain that would come from facing the truth about themselves or the world around them. Others see them as they are and wonder how they can be oblivious to the facts. Those in this category may weather storms that seem formidable to more realistic types, although one wonders if they have somehow missed hearing that a storm was going on. They are also frequently represented in the letters to the editor section of the school papers at places such as BYU and Ricks College, where such shock is occasionally expressed that someone or some part of the institution has fallen short of perfection. The writer is usually aghast—surely this couldn't happen at "the Lord's university," they say.

Surprising as it may seem to this group, the work of the Church and the work in our homes is all done by imperfect people. Elder Richard L. Evans once said those who will only work with perfect people will soon be all alone. He might have added that even then they will not be with perfect people.

While we should not look excessively at the negative side of things, the Lord does expect us to accept and deal with the realities we see. As he said to Moroni, "And if men come unto me I will show unto them their weakness. . . . I will show unto the Gentiles their weakness, and I will show unto them that faith, hope and charity bringeth unto me—the fountain of all righteousness." (Ether 12:27-28.)

Being realistic about our limitations will make us face some questions and some facts that leave us uncomfortable. But that very discomfort can motivate us toward real growth. As has been said by President Harold B. Lee, the true Church is intended not only to comfort the afflicted, but to afflict the comfortable.

One wonders which is worse — honesty without ideals, or ideals without honesty. Both impede growth and change, both are only a partial view of the entire picture of reality.

In a more specific doctrinal sense, the Lord's invitation to come unto him and let him show us our weaknesses is an important step along the pathway toward faith, hope, and charity. That path leads finally to the "fountain" — the source — of righteousness, which is Jesus Christ. (See Ether 12:28.) One of the blessings of grace along that path is the gift of hope, which is a source of comfort and strength for those who move courageously forward toward the perfecting ideal of the Savior. As put plainly and powerfully by the prophet Jacob, "Wherefore, we search the prophets, and we have many revelations and the spirit of prophecy; and having all these witnesses we obtain a *hope*, and our faith becometh unshaken, insomuch that we truly can command in the name of Jesus and the very trees obey us, or the mountains, or the waves of the sea. Nevertheless, *the Lord God showeth us our weakness that we may know that it is by his grace,* and his great condescensions unto the children of men, that we have power to do these things." (Jacob 4:6-7; emphasis added.)

Moroni spoke of this same gift of hope in this way, "Wherefore, whoso believeth in God might with surety hope for a better world, yea, even a place at the right hand of God, which hope cometh of faith, maketh an anchor to the souls of men, which would make them sure and steadfast, always abounding in good works, being led to glorify God." (Ether 12:4.)

This is the spiritual endowment of hope — of perspective, of patience, of an inner serenity, a sure inner sight, that is "not weary in well-doing." (D&C 64:33.) Such hope is bestowed by the power of the Holy Ghost, "which Comforter filleth with hope." (Moroni 8:26.) It is the hope of which Nephi wrote in explaining the process that follows our entry by baptism into the straight and narrow path: "Wherefore, ye must press forward with a steadfastness in Christ, having a perfect brightness of hope and a love of God and of all men." (2 Nephi 31:20.)

It is the hope that Mormon recognized as a sustaining, God-given source of strength in the maturing stages of spiritual development: "I would speak unto you that are of the church, that are the peaceable followers of Christ, and that have obtained a sufficient hope by which ye can enter into the rest of the Lord. . . . My brethren, I judge these things of you because of your peaceable walk with the children of men." (Moroni 7:3-4.) Not perfect, not frantic; not pessimistic and not artificially cheerful. The walk of those who walk with the endowment of hope is "peaceable."

The practical effect of the endowment of hope is illustrated by the Lord's blessing to Alma and his followers, who were in bondage and were made to carry heavy physical burdens. Alma and his people pleaded with the Lord for help, and he responded: "The burdens which were laid upon Alma and his brethren were made light; yea, the Lord did strengthen them that they could bear up their burdens with ease." (Mosiah 24:15.) The Lord intervened in this way, "that they might know of a surety that I, the Lord God, do visit my people in their afflictions." (Mosiah 24:14.)

It helps us see the place of hope to know that our development toward spiritual maturity is a process, not an event. It is a distance race, not a sprint. It is thus no race for the short-winded.

There was once a young woman who was very much overweight.[3] For her height and build, her ideal weight was 120, but she weighed 200 pounds. She tried every dieting program she could find, and nothing seemed to work. Finally, she came across an unusually promising approach and decided to "go for it" in the greatest effort of her life. To mark the beginning and the seriousness of her commitment, she confided in her bishop and asked for his interest and support.

She lived with her sister in a small apartment. The day the new diet began, she explained to her sister what she was doing. She would help prepare meals and help clean up the kitchen, but she did not want to have access to the refrigerator by herself. She produced a huge chain she had just purchased at a hardware store and wrapped it around the refrigerator. A heavy padlock fastened the two ends of the chain in place. After making sure the padlock was locked, she gave the key to her sister and asked her to hide it. Then, on a whim, she followed her sister to see where the key was hidden. She thought it would strengthen her resolve if she knew where it was and yet chose not to use it.

After several long, weary months, she achieved an exciting milestone — she weighed in at 150 pounds. She ran home that evening to tell her sister the big news, but her sister was out for the evening. She tossed herself into an easy chair and began reflecting on her arduous journey. Her eye caught a glance at the refrigerator in the nearby kitchen, and as she saw the chain around it, she burst into laughter. That is so ridiculous, she thought, but it worked. Then it occurred to her that perhaps a little celebration was in order. So she found the key, unlocked the padlock, unwrapped the heavy chain, and peeked into the icebox. There she found a large new carton of her favorite ice cream. She spooned out a taste and flipped on the television. Then she decided she really did deserve a little celebration, so she filled a dish with the ice cream and sat down to enjoy it in front of the TV. A half hour went by, and she was engrossed in a favorite show. Suddenly, as the show ended, she discovered she had just finished off the entire half gallon of ice cream.

At that point she burst into tears and was inconsolable. She frantically called her bishop, raced to his home, and confessed in tears as though she had committed an unpardonable sin. She wailed that she obviously had no self-control. There was no point in trying to continue, now or ever.

Her wise bishop calmly replied, "Look how far you've come! You've lost fifty pounds!" Then he counseled her with a ringing central message: Dieting is a process, not an event. She only needed to regain her perspective and, thereby, her hope.

So it is with our spiritual development. To develop toward a Christlike character is a process, not an event. There may one day be some crowning event, in which the final endowment of grace completes a process that may take longer than mortal life. But to qualify for such a conclusion requires patience and persistence more than it requires flawlessness. It is, indeed, our own groping and reaching in the struggle for growth that qualifies us for divine help. Reid Nibley described this process in these lines:

A distant star
But not too far
To lure us out into the firmament
And tho we ne'er may reach it,
We have tried.
And in the trying
Have learned, perchance,
To make an orbit of our own.

Our effort to reach for the distant star of the ideal, of what ought to be, is much like the massive effort required to allow a space rocket to break through the forceful pull of gravity. But our own orbit awaits us beyond the edge of gravity.

The divine blessing of hope gives us much-needed perspective and strengthens our will to keep moving, against the odds, against the backward pull. It is the principle by which our Father guides us — line upon line, precept upon precept. It is, "Lead, kindly light, amid the encircling gloom. . . . I do not ask to see the distant scene; one step enough for me."

And as we expand the reach of our circle of reality, the strangest thing happens: The circle of the ideal recedes to the horizon, creating both new aspirations and a new gap. We are like a toddler just learning to walk. A parent kneels a few steps away and coaxes with outstretched hands: "You can do it; come to mommy!" Just as the toddler is about to arrive, the parent might move back a step or two, stretching the toddler's reach beyond his grasp.

Our Father in Heaven also waits and coaxes and literally gives us hope—and something about the perspective of hope maintains in our vision an optimal distance between the ideal and the real. When our capacities are small, God's expectations are not very demanding—as with some commandments that are "adapted to the capacity of the weak and the weakest of all saints, who are or can be called saints." (D&C 89:3.) But just as we master these elementary demands, we discover greater expectations that we didn't quite see before. Gradually our capacity grows, but so does our understanding of what more we must become. "For of him unto whom much is given much is required." (D&C 82:3.) The Lord would have us stretch—but not out of shape. As Elder Neal A. Maxwell has said, the soul is like a violin string—it makes music only when it is being stretched.

In the midst of this process, the blessing of hope keeps the gap at a manageable distance. Our perceptions and attitudes really can be shaped and lifted by a gift of divinely given insight that lets us feel, even with some anticipation and optimism, that we can do it. This gift of hope lets us focus confidently on steps that are within reach, but still something of a stretch. If the ideal were too close to the real in our perspective, we would be less inclined to reach to the limits of our capacity. If the ideal seemed too far away from where we are, we would be too discouraged even to try; things would just seem too hopeless.

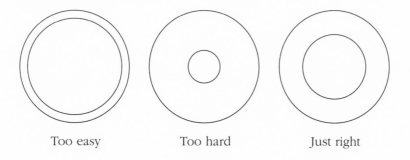

Too easy   Too hard   Just right

187

Hope, a divinely given blessing of atoning grace for those who seek it, after all they can do on their own, establishes in the way our mind sees things just the right distance between where we are and where we strive to be. It also reassures us, somehow, that the ever-receding ideal is not a trick, but part of a growth process that can be not only acceptable but exhilarating. The growing pains become a sign of life and energy, and we are invigorated by hope to watch each step unfold. For the hope within our heart is the Spirit of the Almighty: "For I will go before your face. I will be on your right hand and on your left, and my Spirit shall be in your hearts, and mine angels round about you, to bear you up." (D&C 84:88.)

CHAPTER ELEVEN

Charity and the Tree of Life

T he dictionary defines charity as "performing benevolent actions for the needy with no expectation of material reward," or as "something given to persons in need." These definitions are reflected in our calling such institutions as churches and hospitals "charitable" organizations, meaning vehicles through which service to the needy is rendered. The similar term *Christian service* is often associated with charitable acts, whether performed by individuals or organizations.

With these terms in mind, some people in past years have criticized the Church and its members with the claim that many of them are so preoccupied with "Church work" that they seldom render true Christian service. I once heard a provocative speech by a devoted Latter-day Saint who believed the Church should have committees on social justice and Christian service, in addition to committees on home teaching and missionary work. He shared several unsettling illustrations describing Church members who confined their service-oriented activities to interaction with other Church members or who showed insensitivity and lack of concern for nonmembers as neighbors, associates, or simply as other human beings.

I recall during my graduate school days reading an article in a national magazine that expressed concern about "the rel-

189

evance of Mormonism," suggesting that "Mormonism is too much concerned with the perfection of its own organization, too little with the problems of the world."[1] At the time I read this article, I was also becoming aware of an emerging emphasis among the intellectual leadership of the American Protestant and Catholic churches toward greater "social relevance" for institutional Christianity. That emphasis has become a major movement during the past quarter century, as Christian ministers and theologians in most denominations — including most recently the Conference of Catholic Bishops in the United States — have turned significant institutional attention toward the problems of equality, social justice, war, poverty, and other social issues.

I have been heartened to sense an increasing awareness of and concern about such issues among individual Church members in recent years. I sense that LDS college students have a higher sense of social obligation than they did a generation ago; the Church's youth activity programs are emphasizing the importance of service projects and the need to support minority people, the handicapped, the elderly, and other disadvantaged groups; the Church welfare program, including fast offerings, and the home teaching and visiting teaching programs regularly involve thousands of Church members in reaching out to the needy. When the Church a few years ago reduced its local meeting schedules to a three-hour block on Sundays, the First Presidency told Church members that the change would free up precious Sunday time for individual and family Christian service. General Church leaders are increasingly urging local leaders to spend their time "ministering" to personal needs rather than only "administering" their assignments.

There is an ample doctrinal foundation to support these developments. For one thing, although Christ's followers are not of the world, they are deliberately *in* it. And, as Oliver Wendell Holmes once said, "It is required of man that he share the action and the passion of his time, at the peril of being judged not to have lived." More fundamentally, King Benjamin told his people, "When ye are in the service of your fellow beings ye are only in the service of your God." (Mosiah 2:17.) The Savior taught his followers that his Father's kingdom would be inherited by those who had fed *him* when he was hungry, clothed him when he was naked, and visited him when sick or in prison. But when asked, "When saw we thee an hungred, and fed thee? or thirsty, and gave thee drink?" he said, "Inasmuch as ye have done it unto one of the least of these my brethren, ye have done it unto me." (See Matthew 25:34-40.) As Joseph Smith thought of losing his life in Carthage Jail, he yearned for the singing of "A Poor Wayfaring Man of Grief," which poignantly sets the theme of Matthew 25:34-40 to music.

Yet the Church as an institution has not been significantly involved in the momentum of recent national movements that seek to make religion more socially relevant. Nor has there been any large institutional step in the Church to turn our attention away from the traditional emphasis on families, scripture study, missionary work, and genealogy, even though service to others is becoming an increasingly emphasized theme. The counsel of Church leaders regarding political and social causes has similarly reflected a preference for individual involvement, according to the judgment of the members in their own local situations.

I have wondered at times why this institutional sense of priorities has continued over the past two or three decades of intense social and political ferment in the United States and elsewhere. Several possible reasons come to mind. For one thing, the worldwide nature of the Church makes it impossible to provide direction from Church headquarters regarding the social and political circumstances in each country where Church members live. In addition, sensitivities about Church-state relationships make it generally more appropriate for Church members to become individually involved in potential political issues. Moreover, the resources of the Church are limited, making it necessary to focus on needs of the highest possible potential. But why would our theology dictate giving high priority to missionary work, temples, and meetinghouses? The answer is, not surprisingly, a theological one. It suggests that the three-fold mission of the Church — preaching the gospel, perfecting the Saints, and redeeming the dead — is perhaps the ultimate social action program.

To explore this theological foundation, a question about the first and second great commandments is in order. The Savior taught that love for God was the greatest commandment, and the second was like unto it — love for neighbor. "On these two commandments hang all the law and the prophets." (Matthew 22:40.) Our relationships with God and with our fellowman might be represented as follows:

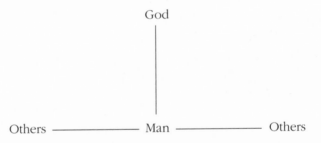

The vertical axis in this diagram represents our relationship with God. The horizontal axis represents our relationships with other people. In which of these two relationships is true charity to be found?

It could reasonably be assumed that charity is obviously located along the horizontal axis, because the very nature of charity is love of neighbor. Even "pure religion" itself consists mostly of such horizontal level acts as "to visit the fatherless and widows in their affliction." (James 1:27.) But further inquiry suggests a less obvious answer.

When Paul wrote about charity in his famous letter to the Corinthians ("Though I speak with the tongues of men and of angels, and have not charity, I am become as sounding brass, or a tinkling cymbal." — 1 Corinthians 13:1), he said, "And though I bestow all my goods to feed the poor . . . and have not charity, it profiteth me nothing." (1 Corinthians 13:3.) How could one give away all his possessions without having charity? What could be more charitable than giving all one's goods to feed the poor?

In a celebrated sermon to teachers in the Church Educational System some years ago, President J. Reuben Clark raised a similar question:

> The teaching of a system of ethics to the students is not a sufficient reason for running our seminaries and institutes. . . . To make of the Gospel a mere system of ethics is to confess a lack of faith, if not disbelief, in the hereafter. . . . One living, burning honest testimony of a righteous God-fearing man that Jesus is the Christ and that Joseph was God's prophet is worth a thousand books and lectures aimed at debasing the Gospel to a system of ethics. . . . [2]

What could be more religious than ethical standards and ethical relationships with other people? Yet both Paul and President Clark saw that the heart of the religious life — even including the charitable and ethical fruits of true religion — is ultimately to be found not along the horizontal axis but in our personal relationship with God.

Let us further explore the theological foundation of this idea. The scriptures teach us about two trees — the tree of knowledge and the tree of life. The most complete description of the tree of knowledge is found in the story of Adam and Eve. The most complete description of the tree of life is found in the story of Lehi's dream in the Book of Mormon. Lehi described his partaking of the fruit of the tree of life as follows: "And as I partook of the fruit thereof it filled my soul with exceedingly great joy; *wherefore, I began to be desirous* that my family should partake of it also; for I knew that it was desirable above all other fruit." (1 Nephi 8:12.) This tree of life represents "the love of God, which sheddeth itself abroad in the hearts of the children of men; wherefore, it is the most desirable above all things." (1 Nephi 11:22.) Lehi's experience was at the summit of the vertical axis. His relationship with God came to its point of highest fulfillment as he partook of God's love. Yet in that very moment, as God's love "sheddeth itself" in his heart, he "began to be desirous" for his family.

A grandson of Lehi named Enos had what seems to be a remarkably similar experience. Enos was alone in the forest when the words he had heard from his father, Jacob, "concerning eternal life, and the joy of the saints, sunk deep into my heart. And my soul hungered; and I . . . cried unto [God] in mighty prayer and supplication for mine own soul." (Enos 1:3-4.) Enos received a manifestation in which his sins were forgiven because of his faith in Christ. As the Lord gave Enos this overwhelming assurance, Enos then *"began to feel a desire for the welfare of my brethren, the Nephites; wherefore, I did pour out my whole soul unto God for them."* (Enos 1:9; emphasis added.) In answer to his fervent petitioning in behalf of his people, the Lord made some great promises to Enos that resulted in preserving the scriptural record for their benefit. Just as Lehi "began to be desirous" for the welfare of others, so did Enos begin "to feel a desire" for others in the very moment of fulfillment in his personal relationship with God.

Following their own miraculous conversion, Alma and the sons of Mosiah developed a great desire to preach the gospel as missionaries. The description of their feelings bears clear resemblance to the experiences of Lehi and Enos: "Now they were desirous that salvation should be declared to every creature, for they could not bear that any human soul should perish; yea, even the very thoughts that any soul should endure endless torment did cause them to quake and tremble. *And thus did the Spirit of the Lord work upon them. . . .* "(Mosiah 28:3-4.) In his own later account of the same experience, Alma described his having "been born of God." From that time forward, he "labored without ceasing, that I might bring souls unto re-

194

pentance; that I might bring them to taste of the exceeding joy of which I did taste; that they might also be born of God, and be filled with the Holy Ghost." (Alma 36:24.)

From these personal accounts we learn that complete harmony with God along the vertical religious axis leads directly to deep and perhaps permanent feelings of concern for others along the horizontal religious axis. The nature and source of this feeling of concern for others is revealed in Mormon's sublime language at the conclusion of his sermon to the members of the Church on faith, hope, and charity:

> But charity is the pure love of Christ, and it endureth forever; and whoso is found possessed of it at the last day, it shall be well with him.
>
> Wherefore, my beloved brethren, pray unto the Father with all the energy of heart, that ye may be filled with this love, which he hath bestowed upon all who are true followers of his Son, Jesus Christ; that ye may become the sons of God; that when he shall appear we shall be like him, for we shall see him as he is; that we may have this hope; that we may be purified even as he is pure. Amen. (Moroni 7:47-48.)

The "true followers" of Jesus who "pray with all the energy of heart" are here given the assurance that they may one day be "filled with this love" called charity, which is the very same "love which [the Lord] hast had for the children of men." (Ether 12:34.) We apparently cannot develop a complete and permanent Christlike love for other people on our own, even though we must qualify as "true followers of his son" in order to receive this love. To be sure, our own internally generated compassion for the needs of others is a crucial indication of our desire to be followers of the Savior—clearly part of "all we can do." For that reason, we must be reaching out to others even as we reach out to God, rather than waiting to respond to others' needs until our charitable instincts are quickened by the Spirit. But even then, charity in its full-blown sense is *"bestowed* upon" Christ's righteous followers. Its source, like all other blessings of the Atonement, is the grace of God: "I prayed unto the Lord that he would give unto the Gentiles grace, that they might have charity." (Ether 12:36.)

The purpose of charity, however, is not merely to cause a proper motivation for charitable acts toward other people — though that is of course one important result. The ultimate purpose is to make Christ's followers *like him*: "He hath bestowed [this love] upon all who are true followers of his Son, Jesus Christ; *that ye may become the sons of God;* that when he shall appear *we shall be like him* . . . that we may be purified even as he is pure." (Moroni 7:48; emphasis added.)

To partake fully of the tree of life is thus to be given the nature of Christ. Those so blessed as to receive this bestowal of the Savior's own character and attributes are filled with charity, because charity is central to the divine nature. The totality of the blessing, however, is complete, sanctified perfection: "Yea, come unto Christ, and be perfected in him. . . . then are ye sanctified in Christ by the grace of God." (Moroni 10:32-33.)

The ultimate purpose of the gospel of Jesus Christ is to cause the sons and daughters of God to become as Christ is. Those who see religious purpose only in terms of ethical service in the relationship between man and fellowmen may miss that divinely ordained possibility. It is quite possible to render charitable — even "Christian" — service without developing deeply ingrained and permanent Christlike character. Paul understood this when he warned against giving all one's goods to feed the poor without true charity. President Clark understood it when he warned against equating man-made systems of ethics with the gospel of Christ. We can give without loving, but we cannot love without giving. If our vertical relationship with God is complete, then, by the fruit of that relationship, the horizontal relationship with our fellow beings will also be complete. We then act charitably toward others, not merely

196

because we think we should, but because that is the way we are.

Service to others will surely bring us closer to God, especially when motivated by an unselfish sense of personal compassion. But even such desirable service will not of itself complete our relationship with God, because it will not by itself result in the bestowal of the complete attributes of godliness. That bestowal requires the ordinances and doctrines of the restored gospel and all the other elements of sacrifice and obedience spelled out in the scriptures. For that reason, while religious philosophies whose highest aim is social relevance may do much good, they will not ultimately lead people to achieve the highest religious purpose, which is to become as God and Christ are. It is even possible that an ethical philosophy grounded totally in a secular concern for the temporal welfare of others — desirable as that is in proper context — can by subtle logic even undermine the role of true religion. A limited ethical sense may artificially and temporarily imitate the fruits of true charity while at the same time making the pursuit of a fully developed relationship with God appear to be self-centered and, therefore, unworthy of a true Christian.

In addition, religious or ethical systems whose highest good is social justice do not necessarily provide the members of a society with the opportunity for personal, individualized development of true religious character. Indeed, such systems may impede the development of individual character by assuming that man's nature is fixed — either good or bad — and that institutional religion as a change agent should devote its attention to healing broad-scale social ills rather than to personal development. The restored gospel has a loftier and longer range purpose than this, which is empowered by forces that can change and develop the individual to the point of also solving social problems in permanent ways through the aggregation of personal solutions. Obviously, some minimal but significant level of political liberty and economic capacity are necessary for the gospel to achieve this promise, but the process of development caused by acceptance of the gospel must finally become an individual process.

Even keeping the commandments, desirable as that is, is not an end in itself. He that "receiveth a commandment with doubtful heart, and keepeth it with slothfulness, the same is damned." (D&C 58:29.) This is because the Lord's commandments are designed to develop the individual toward the capacity and spiritual state of mind needed to receive a perfected nature. Thus it may be relatively unimportant just how many white marks may be chalked up against some number of black marks over the course of one's life. Righteous acts in the past of an essentially evil person will not change what he or she has become. In the same way, disobedient acts in the past of an essentially righteous person will not change what he or she has become. What we are is more important than what we know or what we do. The Savior did not say, "*Know* ye therefore perfect" or "*Do* ye therefore perfect"; he said "*Be* ye therefore perfect."

This sense of *becoming* suggests that obedience and repentance are meaningful because they encourage the development of the spiritual maturity necessary to love God with all our might, mind, and strength. It also explains why the pursuit of knowledge and understanding by our own experience in a lone and dreary world, regardless of our errors, our disappointments, our failures and our confusion, would be the course designed by God for our ultimate preparation. After sufficient human experience, with all its variety and complexity, coupled with a meek and lowly heart inclined fully toward obedient striving, we have tasted the bitter in such a way that we know to prize the good. Then are we ready to grasp the meaning of the godlike life his grace so much desires to bestow, which includes an unbounded commitment to the welfare of others. Then we are prepared to enter into his presence. "To him that overcometh will I give to eat of the tree of life, which is in the midst of the paradise of God." (Revelation 2:7.)

When that day comes, we will be given the quality or nature

of life that God himself has, which is called "eternal" (godlike) life. It is an endowment of pure grace, the greatest endowment of all: "And, if you keep my commandments and endure to the end you shall have eternal life, which gift is the greatest of all the gifts of God." (D&C 14:7.)

This tree of life is the same tree of which Adam and Eve were not allowed to partake until they had faithfully and obediently endured the trials of mortal experience to the point of offering God a broken heart and a contrite spirit. It is the tree described as growing from the seed of faith Alma describes in Alma 32. It is the tree whose fruit represents the final bestowal of not only all that the Father has but what the Father is. No wonder that, when Lehi partook of this "love of God, which sheddeth itself abroad in the hearts of the children of men," he declared it was "the most desirable above all things." And an angel added, "Yea, and the most joyous to the soul." (1 Nephi 11:22-23.)

Epilogue

I. The Tree of the Knowledge of Good and Evil

> *And the Lord God planted a garden eastward in Eden; and there he put the man whom he had formed. And out of the ground made the Lord God to grow . . . the tree of life . . . in the midst of the garden, and the tree of knowledge of good and evil.* (Genesis 2:8-9.)

Eve walked in the garden in the cool of the day. The serpent saw her as she walked and he sought to beguile her, for he knew not the mind of God. The garden was beautiful, but Eve did not realize how beautiful it was, for she was innocent.

The serpent spoke to the woman. Behold, he said, *the tree of the knowledge of good and evil.* Eve looked at him and wondered who he was. Eat of this tree, said the serpent, for in the day you eat thereof shall your eyes be opened, and you shall be as the gods, knowing good and evil. Eve looked at *the tree of the knowledge of good and evil.* It appeared pleasant to her eyes and its fruit seemed desirable to make one wise. The serpent said, eat. Eve did eat, and also gave unto her husband, and he did eat. And their eyes were opened.

Adam and Eve walked together in the garden in the cool of the day. The garden seemed more beautiful now. They

201

clasped their hands together as they walked. Eve was glad she was not alone. They looked toward the midst of the garden not far away and saw *the tree of life*. Adam wondered what this tree could be. Of a sudden, they heard the voice of the Lord God, and they hid themselves among the trees of the garden.

The Lord God said unto the woman and the man, What is this thing which you have done? Because you have eaten of the forbidden fruit, you cannot remain in the garden. You must be cast out. Cursed now shall be the ground for your sake; in sorrow shall you eat of it all the days of your life. You may now have children, but only in great sorrow. Now you may have joy, but only in the midst of misery and woe.

The Lord God said to his Only Begotten, who was with him, The man and woman are become as one of us, for now they will know good and evil. But let them not yet partake of *the tree of life*, or they will have no space to repent and prepare themselves to become as we are. Let them taste the bitter that they may know to prize the good.

The man and woman were driven out of the garden, and they brought forth children, even the family of all the earth.

II. The Tree of Life

> And to bring about his eternal purposes in the end of man, after he had created our first parents, ... it must needs be that there was an opposition; even the forbidden fruit in opposition to the tree of life; the one being sweet and the other bitter.
> (2 Nephi 2:15.)

Adam began to till the earth in the heat of the day. He felt the sweat drip down his face. He paused to wipe his brow and looked up at the sun. He looked back down at the fertile earth and thought about the angel who had come to him early that morning as he offered up a sacrifice to God. He had not known why God commanded him to offer sacrifices, but the angel taught him: This thing is a similitude of the sacrifice of the Only Begotten of the Father, which is full of grace and truth.

Adam and his wife called upon God and betimes heard his voice. But they could not see him, for they were shut out from his presence. God gave them commandments and they obeyed.

One day God spoke to Adam, saying he should be baptized and should teach his children of repentance and baptism. Adam wanted to understand and so he asked why. The Lord God said, I have forgiven your transgression in the garden, and now it is given to you, that you may know good from evil. When your children grow up, sin will conceive in their hearts, and they will taste the bitter, that they may know to prize the good; wherefore, they may choose, for they are agents unto themselves. But they must repent of their sins and be baptized or they cannot inherit the kingdom of God, for no unclean thing can dwell there. As you have fallen, you may be redeemed, together with all your children, even as many as will.

Adam understood. He fell in humility to the earth and said, Blessed be the name of God, for because of my transgression my eyes are opened and in this life I shall have joy. Eve heard his words, she understood them, and she was glad.

After many years, the Lord God gave a dream to a son of Adam called Lehi, in which Lehi beheld *the tree of life*, whose fruit was desirable to make one happy. As he partook of the fruit, it was sweet above all he had ever before tasted, and it filled his soul with exceeding great joy.

Lehi was old and full of sorrow for his children. He had been faithful in the midst of many trials. As he tasted the sweet fruit of *the tree of life*, he prized it with all his soul. Then he began to feel a desire for the welfare of his children, that they might partake of it also. The Lord God gave these feelings to Lehi, for the tree was the love that God has for the children of men, and which he bestows as an act of grace upon all who are true followers of Jesus, his Son. By this means, these followers take upon themselves his divine nature.

The fruit of *the tree of life* is the most desirable of all things, and the most joyous to the soul. If Adam and Eve had partaken of this fruit immediately after partaking of the fruit of knowledge, the plan of salvation would have been frustrated, for they would have had no preparatory state. But they were true and faithful, laboring all their days together and wading through much affliction and sorrow. They fulfilled their part in the great plan of happiness, until one day they again saw the face of the Lord God and embraced him with pleasure. Then he said unto them, Come unto me, ye blessed, there is a place prepared for you in the mansions of my Father. And thus did Adam and Eve, Lehi and Sariah, and their faithful children become as God and Christ are, to live with them forever in the fulness of eternal life.[1]

Notes

INTRODUCTION

The Atonement Is Not Just for Sinners

1. *Newsweek*, September 1, 1980, page 68.
2. Robert A. Rhees, "Letter to the Editor," *Sunstone*, January/February 1981, page 2.
3. Ibid.
4. Boyd K. Packer, "Atonement, Agency, Accountability," *Ensign*, May 1988, pages 69-70.
5. Daniel H. Ludlow, "The Relationship between Grace and Works," *Supplement: A Symposium on the New Testament* (Church Educational System, 1984), page 29. The one article on grace was Gerald N. Lund, "Salvation, By Grace or By Works?" *Ensign*, April 1981, page 16. Since 1983, the Church periodicals have published at least two other articles on the subject of grace: Elder Gene R. Cook, "Christmas Is a Time for Rejoicing in the Grace of the Lord," *New Era*, December 1988, page 4; and Colin B. Douglas, "What I've Learned about Grace Since Coming Down from the Sycamore Tree," *Ensign*, April 1989, page 12.
6 Bruce R. McConkie, "What Think Ye of Salvation by Grace?" *BYU 1983-84 Fireside and Devotional Speeches*, page 44.
7. *Ensign*, May 1988, page 69.
8. Hugh Nibley has said that "people are usually surprised to learn that *atonement*, an accepted theological term, is neither from a Greek nor a Latin word, but is good old English and really does mean, when we write it out, at-one-ment, denoting both a state of being one with another and the process by which that end is achieved." From "The Atonement," a talk given in Salt Lake City, November 10, 1988.
9. John A. Widtsoe, *Evidences and Reconciliations*, 3 vols. in 1, arranged by G. Homer Durham (Salt Lake City: Bookcraft, 1960), page 193.
10. These references to Job are cited and developed more fully in chapter six.
11. Neal A. Maxwell, *Not My Will, But Thine* (Salt Lake City: Bookcraft, 1988), page 51.

12. G. Kittel, *Theological Dictionary of the New Testament*, vol. 1 (Grand Rapids: Eerdsmans, 1964), page 271. I am indebted to Jack Welch at Brigham Young University for calling my attention to this material.
13. Ibid., pages 273-74.
14. Ibid.
15. Ibid., pages 296, 297.
16. Ibid., pages 290-300.

Prologue

1. T. S. Eliot, *Four Quartets* (London: The Folio Society, 1968), page 55.
2. William Shakespeare, *MacBeth*, Act V, Scene V.
3. Section III of the Prologue draws upon Moses 4; Alma 32; Alma 1; Nephi 11; 2 Nephi 9; 2 Nephi 25; 3 Nephi 9; Hebrews 2; Hebrews 5; Isaiah 53; and John 17. See also James E. Talmage, *Jesus the Christ* (Salt Lake City: The Church of Jesus Christ of Latter-day Saints, 1949), page 669.

CHAPTER ONE
The Life Cycle of Adam and Eve

1. The concept on which this cycle is based draws loosely upon Edward F. Edinger, *Ego and Archetype* (New York: Penguin Books, 1972), page 41. I am indebted to Larry Thompson at Ricks College for calling my attention to Edinger's work.
2. Christopher Lasch, *Haven in a Heartless World* (New York: Basic Books, 1977), pages 123, 125, 186.
3. Ibid.

CHAPTER TWO
Entering the Life Cycle

1. Joseph Smith, *Lectures on Faith* (Salt Lake City: Deseret Book, 1985 edition). See "Lecture Sixth."
2. See the Prologue.

CHAPTER THREE
Opposition and Joy

1. "Blessed art thou, Joseph. Behold, thou art little; wherefore hearken unto the words of thy brother, Nephi." (2 Nephi 3:25.)
2. Friedrich Zaugg, "How I Got to Zion," *Der Stern*, vol. 34 (1902), page 60.
3. Marie Hafen, address delivered at Ricks College Devotional, January 15, 1985.
4. Robert Browning, "Paracelsus," emphasis added.
5. Quoted from an unknown author in Spencer W. Kimball, *Faith Precedes the Miracle* (Salt Lake City: Deseret Book Co., 1979), page 99.

CHAPTER FOUR
A Willingness to Learn from Pain

1. *Time*, February 5, 1973, page 35.
2. "O My Father," *Hymns* (Salt Lake City: The Church of Jesus Christ of Latter-day Saints, 1985), number 292.

CHAPTER FIVE
Two Cheers for Excellence

1. Ernest Renan, *History of the People of Israel* (1891), page 415.
2. Donald Kagen, et. al., *The Western Heritage* (New York: MacMillan, 2d ed., 1983), page 46.
3. Herbert Wallace Schneider, *The Puritan Mind* (Ann Arbor: The University of Michigan Press, 1958), pages 34-35.
4. Robert R. Palmer and Joel Colton, *A History of the Modern World* (New York: Alfred A. Knopf, 1963), page 75.
5. Thomas Greer, *A Brief History of the Western World* (New York: Harcourt Brace Jovanovich, 4th ed., 1983), page 458.
6. Boyd K. Packer, "The Choice," *Ensign*, November 1980, page 21.
7. Joseph F. Smith, *Gospel Doctrine* (Salt Lake City: Deseret Book Co., 1949), page 285.
8. Merlin Myers, "The Morality of Kinship," address delivered at Brigham Young University, November 15, 1983.
9. "Lecture Sixth," *Lectures on Faith*.
10. *Dialogue*, vol. 8, no. 1, page 75.
11. From Robert Louis Stevenson, "The Lantern-Bearers," quoted in William James, "On a Certain Blindness in Human Beings," *Talks to Teachers on Psychology and to Students on Some of Life's Ideals* (Cambridge, Massachusetts: Harvard University Press, 1983), pages 135-36.
12. Ibid.

CHAPTER SIX
Obedience, Sacrifice, and a Contrite Spirit

1. "Lecture Sixth," *Lectures on Faith*.

CHAPTER SEVEN
Human Nature and Learning by Experience

1. See chapter nine.
2. Herbert W. Schneider, *The Puritan Mind* (1930), page 98.
3. Widtsoe, *Evidences and Reconciliations*, page 193.
4. See Bruce C. Hafen, "The Value of the Veil," *The Believing Heart* (Salt Lake City: Bookcraft, 1986), page 49.
5. Ibid., page 52.
6. Michael Polanyi, *Personal Knowledge* (New York: Harper and Row, 1964), page 53.

CHAPTER EIGHT
Justice, Mercy, and Rehabilitation

1. "When thou art in tribulation, and all these things are come upon thee, even in the latter days, if thou turn to the Lord thy God, and shalt be obedient unto his voice; (*For the Lord thy God is a merciful God;*) he will not forsake thee, neither destroy thee, nor forget the covenant of thy fathers which he sware unto them." (Deuteronomy 4:30-31; emphasis added.)

2. "Grace," Dictionary of the LDS Edition of the King James Version of the Bible, page 697.
3. Sometimes we assume that only those who repent will return to the presence of God; however, the scriptures teach that each person will return to God's presence for the purpose of being judged. The obedient will then remain in his presence, but those who were disobedient and nonrepentant in mortality will, following their judgment, be shut out from his presence in a second spiritual death. See Helaman 14:15-18 and Mormon 9:12-14.
4. See Francis A. Allen, *The Decline of the Rehabilitative Ideal* (New Haven: Yale University Press, 1981).
5. See Spencer W. Kimball, *The Miracle of Forgiveness* (Salt Lake City: Bookcraft, 1969), pages 191-200.
6. Ibid., pages 196-200.

CHAPTER NINE
Grace and the Higher Law

1. See, for example, Deuteronomy 6:5 ("And thou shalt love the Lord thy God with all thine heart, and with all thy soul, and with all thy might.") and the affirmative thrust of the fifth commandment, "Honor thy father and thy mother." (Exodus 20:12.)
2. See chapter ten.
3. See chapter eleven.

CHAPTER TEN
Hope

1. Albert Ellis, "Psychotherapy and Atheistic Values," *Journal of Consulting and Clinical Psychology* (1980), pages 635, 637.
2. Allen, *The Decline of the Rehabilitative Ideal,* page 28.
3. I first heard this story from Victor Cline.

CHAPTER ELEVEN
Charity and the Tree of Life

1. *Time*, April 10, 1967.
2. J. Reuben Clark, Jr., "The Chartered Course of the Church in Education," address given August 8, 1938 to Church Seminary and Institute instructors at Aspen Grove, Utah (Salt Lake City: Church Commissioner of Education, 1980).

Epilogue

1. The Epilogue is based on Genesis 1-3; Moses 3-6; 1 Nephi 8, 11; 2 Nephi 2; Enos 1:27; Alma 7:5; Alma 12:26; Alma 42:3-8; and Moroni 7:48.

Index

Accidents, consequences of, 10. *See also* Carelessness

Achievement, personal, 96, 99, 102. *See also* Success

Adam and Eve: Fall of, 7, 10; transgression of, 8, 14, 131, 145; innocence of, 9, 74, 132; obedience and sacrifice of, 30; taught fulness of gospel, 158

Adolescents: judgmental capability of, 44-46; disciplining, 47

Adversity: responsibility for, 11; life cycle and, 51; natural part of life, 57

Agency, Free. *See* Independence, Acts of

Aldous Huxley, 64

Alma the Younger, experience of, 52-53

Approval, desire for, 99, 104

Atonement: pays for more than sin, 1, 8, 15, 20, 22, 29, 104, 121, 138-139, 175; need to teach and understand, 1, 25-26; in scripture, 3; sorrow and, 5, 13; benefits of, 8, 12, 17; first application of, 10; limits of, 13; King Benjamin's

teachings on, 13-14; a practical theory, 25; purpose of, 63; relationship to laws of mercy and justice, 145-46; misunderstanding doctrines of, 150

Bitterness: mortal, 1, 11, 14, 29, 139; enduring, of sin, 54; necessity of, 63-64

Book of Mormon: Atonement in, 3, 26; grace in, 17

Burton, Theodore M., on knowledge in testimony, 73

Butler, Samuel, 148

Calvinism, election and grace in, 4, 96-97

Carelessness. *See* Wrongdoing

Celestial Kingdom, entrance requirements of, 7; Joseph Smith's description of, 17

Charity: gift of, 18-19, 168, 195; defined, 189; purpose of, 196

Choices, unwise, 11

Christianity, social relevance of, 190-91

City of God, 126

About the Author

Bruce C. Hafen was sustained to the First Quorum of the Seventy of The Church of Jesus Christ of Latter-day Saints on April 6, 1996. He was formerly Provost of Brigham Young University and Professor of Law at BYU's J. Reuben Clark Law School. A graduate of Dixie College, BYU, and the University of Utah Law School, he has served as Director of Research and Evaluation for the Correlation Department of the Church, as President of Ricks College, and as Dean of the BYU Law School. In the Church, he has served as a Gospel Doctrine teacher, as a counselor in a bishopric and in a stake presidency, and as a Regional Representative. He is a nationally recognized authority on family law and education law. His numerous articles appear in the *Ensign, Brigham Young Magazine,* and such professional legal journals as *Harvard Law Review* and the *American Bar Association Journal.*

He and his wife, Marie K. Hafen, have seven children and ten grandchildren. Their home is in Orem, Utah.